DEVELOPMENT OF ABILITY TO REASON IN SCHOOL EDUCATION

DEVELOPMENT OF ABILITY TO REASON IN SCHOOL EDUCATION

K.P. GARG

Foreword by

DEVENDRA JOSHI

CONCEPT PUBLISHING COMPANY, NEW DELHI 110059

This publication was financially supported by the National Council of Educational Research and Training (NCERT), New Delhi through a grant.

ISBN 81-7022-398-9

First Published 1992

Published and Printed by
Ashok Kumar Mittal
Concept Publishing Company
A/15-16, Commercial Block, Mohan Garden
NEW DELHI 110059 (India)

Lasertypeset by
Microtech Advance Printing Systems (Pvt.) Ltd.
H-13, Bali Nagar,
NEW DELHI 110015

FOREWORD

ONE OF the major problems of curriculum planners eluding success has been to arrange class-room environment in such a manner that of pupils with a given cognitive structure can learn what they are supposed to learn. This is so because we still do not have definite knowledge about the cognitive structure of pupils at various stages of their development. This is not all. There is so much of inter-regional and intra-regional variations in maturation of cognitive structure that to match learning with cognitive structure remains a mind boggling problem.

Dr. K.P. Garg need to be congratulated for delving into this problem and identifying the reasoning abilities of 14+ children. Much of learning at secondary level of present-day schools depends upon the kind of reasoning abilities that 14+ children have. However due to our pre-occupations with the nature and structure of cognitive abilities and the kind of test that will help us to secure measures for these had led to neglect of role of sampling. Dr. Garg has been able to establish that, if we give attention to this aspect, we may be able to identify the variables in a much more rigorous manner.

I hope this study will be of use both to curriculum planners and to investigators engaged in cognitive studies – the former to work out studies on ability groupings and curriculum efficacy, and the latter to identify their variables much more vigorously.

Dean, Faculty of Education,
Jamia Millia Islamia, New Delhi

DEVENDRA JOSHI

PREFACE

TAKING INTO account the objective of education proposed by various national commissions and committees appointed by the Government of India since Independence, one view which appears to be in common is that education should equip every individual to fulfil his various roles in a society, by providing opportunities for developing his abilities and affective characteristics. In each educational encounter which involves the teacher, the taught and the curriculum, the learner occupies the central position. But the progress or efficiency of the learning varies among students of the same sex, age and grade mainly due to differences in their readiness to learn. This is because they differ in their individual abilities. Among the abilities, the most significant to determine the readiness of an individual to learn, is the cognitive or intellectual ability. Understanding the individual difference among the students in their cognitive or mental ability is, therefore, one of the primary tasks of educators.

Supporters of the theories of cognitive development are of the opinion that understanding of the nature of cognitive structure of the entering abilities is essential to determine the readiness of a child for a terminal task. In order to explore a child's readiness for learning a concept or a principle, Bruner emphasized matching of the cognitive structure of the child with the structure of what is to be taught (Shulman, 1968). Various expert groups constituted by the Government of India, National Council of Educational Research and Training for working out the framework of school curriculum in the country also suggested that for any kind of curriculum planning and innovation, the cognitive structure of the learner has to be taken into account. Thus, there is a need to study the structure of the mental ability of the pupils at different stages of their development before planning out suitable curriculum and other learning experiences.

In view of the available empirical evidence, it appears that one of the significant abilities for scholastic achievement which had been much emphasized in the new Curriculum Framework (1988) and has been thoroughly and widely investigated, happens to be 'reasoning' Reasoning has been a major component of the intelligence tests from the inception of the testing movement. It is interesting to note that the experts who participated in the symposium organized by the editors of the *Journal of Educational Psychology* (1921) did not differentiate much between the concept of Reasoning and General Mental Ability/ Intelligence. All the factor analysts in their theories of mental abilities also found 'Reasoning' a major component. Therefore, it appeared to the author a worthwhile proposition to study the nature of reasoning ability at the age of 14+ when it emerges clearly.

Various efforts have been made in the past to elaborate the concept of reasoning. Induction and deduction were identified as the two aspects of reasoning processes in the traditional studies. Some later studies were a break from the concept of reasoning as induction and deduction, while agreeing with them to some extent. A few of these, in addition to induction and deduction identified some more factors as reasoning abilities. The most fruitful attempt to elaborate the concept of reasoning was made at the University of Southern California by Guilford and his associates (1953, 1954, 1956 and 1959). With the help of factor analyses, Guilford and his associates were able to conceptualize the nature of 'reasoning' in terms of tasks involved in various tests presumed to measure such abilities. However, all these studies were conducted on groups of army or navy recruits, thereby offering no scope for generalisation to various student population. Moreover, average IQ of those army and navy recruits was moderately high with limited range. Thus, they were a highly selected group (homogeneous) and the findings of those studies did not say anything about the heterogeneous groups. Therefore, there was a need to carry out a study to understand the nature of individual differences in 'reasoning ability' for heterogeneous and a homogeneous group of students separately at the age of 14+, when it clearly emerges.

Further, with an over-riding concern to substantiate his SOI model and to achieve invariance of factors, Guilford re-analyzed all the data obtained from the studies on reasoning conducted earlier under the ARP project. This provided him new understanding of the concept of reasoning in terms of the mental processes of cognition and convergent production of his SOI model, which were much broader than the traditional concepts of induction and deduction. One study, mainly to describe the nature of reasoning in terms of mental operations of cognition and convergent productions as suggested by Guilford and four others seeking the relationship of these with scholastic achievement in Science or Mathematics was conducted for student population in India. But this did not encompass all the cognition and convergent production products as posited by Guilford to describe the domain of reasoning with semantic content. This led the author to the identification of the need to study the domain of reasoning by encompassing all the cognition and convergent production products together in one study

On the other hand, the author's attention was drawn to the fact that in one of the five studies conducted in India concerning the domain of reasoning in terms of SOI's mental operations of 'cognition' and 'convergent production', one mixed general, one mixed operations factor, five mixed product factors and one SOI factor emerged; in another, one mixed general factor, two mixed product factors and two SOI factors emerged; in one, three mixed product factors and two SOI factors emerged; in another, five mixed product factors and one SOI factor emerged; in one, one mixed operations factor, one mixed products factor and two SOI factors emerged. When viewed in the light of the debate on the heterogeneity and homogeneity of groups of studies (*cf.* Ch. 2), it appeared to the author that the criteria of sex, age and/or grade level were not sufficient to treat their samples as homogeneous samples. This suggested to him to form two samples, one on the basis of sex, age and grade and another, not only on the basis of sex, age and grade, but also on the basis of social context and maturation of mental ability. In other words, this suggestion to form a heterogeneous and a homogeneous sample in terms of social context and maturation of mental ability, and to study the domain of reasoning separately for them.

To study the above issues in a scientific manner, I found in Dr. D.C. Joshi, Professor and Dean Faculty of Education, Jamia Millia, Islamia, New Delhi a perennial source of encouragement. I therefore, express my deep debt of gratitude to Dr. Joshi without whose constant guidance and help the present work could not have been completed.

I am also greatly indebted to Prof. J.P. Guilford for providing guidance at various stages of development of this study. Infect, Prof. Guilford's theory of Human Intelligence has been a great source of motivation to undertake the present work.

I am very thankful to Shri J.C. Dubey, Senior Lecturer, NCERT for editing the manuscript.

I also express my sincere thanks to Dr.(Mrs.) Girish Bala and

Dr. R.C. Tyagi for allowing me to use the Reasoning Ability tests constructed by them.

I acknowledge with thanks the cooperation and facilities extended by the Principals, and teachers of the schools, the patience and sincere cooperation of the students, in taking tests without which it would not have been possible to collect the data.

I am also thankful to Dr. Sunder Singh, Directorate of Education, Delhi; Mrs. Hema Joshi, Jamia Millia, Islamia, New Delhi; Miss Neeru Garg, Jahangirabad; Prof. H.S. Srivastava, Dean Academic and Head, DMES&DP, NCERT for extending help and cooperation directly or indirectly in completing the present task, and to NCERT for providing the publication grant. I am also grateful to Shri B.S. Nagi, Senior EDP Coordinator, Council for Social Development, Lodi Estate, New Delhi, for extending help in computer programming and processing.

Last, but not the least, I feels overwhelmed in expressing my gratitude to my wife, Mrs. Shanta Garg, who, in spite of her very busy schedule could spare time to be of help to me as and when the necessity arose for completion of this work. My daughters, Seema and Surbhi have also been a source of inspiration in this arduous task.

New Delhi KANTA PRASAD GARG

CONTENTS

LIST OF TABLES

LIST OF FIGURES

1

EDUCATION AND THE COGNITIVE STRUCTURE

IN A democratic set up each person has his unique importance, dignity and merit, both as an individual and as a member of a social group. From the philosophical point of view, each individual is unique and for an educator, issues of an individual's 'being' are as significant and important as those of his 'becoming'. From the psychological point of view, each individual is endowed with a variety of abilities, capacities and capabilities, though, no two schools agree as to which of these are innate and which are acquired through interaction in a social setting. From a sociological point of view, each individual is a dynamic member of several social groups within which he interacts and acquires those capabilities which help him in contributing to mutual welfare and advancement.

Education – An Instrument for Development

After Independence when India took up the challenge of providing social, cultural and economic justice to millions of its people, it not only went about the task of restructuring its socio-political institutions to build a just society, its economic-industrial and agricultural institutions for better utilization of its natural resources, but also of restructuring its educational system in order to develop its human resources for manning these institutions. The first move in this direction was the appointment of University Education Commission in (1948-1949) which considered education, ". . . as the development of body, mind and spirit of each individual with his specific nature" and as, ". . . realisation of potentialities of each individual in the face of actual world of man and things" (Report, Vol. 1, 1-*repr.*, 1962, pp.36-37). Subsequently, accepting "the object of democratic education is the full all-round development of every individual's personality", the

Secondary Education Commission (1952-53) suggested:

> Education should take into account all his needs psychological, emotional and practical – and cater to all of them. The view of education that emerges from this basic concept transcends the narrow academic approach and broadens out into an education for living, i.e., an education to initiate the students into the many-sided art of living in a community.
>
> (Report, VI-*repr*. 1965, pp.20-21)

The Indian Education Commission (1964-66) viewing education as "the one instrument, and one instrument only of change", observed:

> In a democracy, the individual is an end in himself and the primary purpose of education is to provide him with the widest opportunity to develop his potentialities to full. But the path to this goal lies through social reorganization and emphasis on social perspectives. In fact, one of the important principles to be emphasized in the socialistic pattern of society which the nation desires to create, is that individual fulfilment will come, not through selfish and narrow loyalties to personal or group interests, but through the dedication of all to the wider loyalties of national development in all its parameter.
>
> (Report 1966, p.4)

The National Policy on Education (1968) based on the observations and recommendations of the Indian Education Commission (1964-66) while emphasizing radical reconstruction of education essential "for economic and cultural development of the country, for national integration and for realizing the ideal of a socialistic pattern of society", stated:

> The educational system must produce young men and women of character and ability committed to national service and development. Only then will education be able to play its vital role in promoting national progress, creating a sense of common citizenship and culture, and strengthening national integration.
>
> (NPE Resolution, 1968, p.2)

As a sequel to the National Policy Resolution (1968), the Ministry of Education and Social Welfare constituted an expert group in 1973 to develop the curriculum for the 10+2 pattern. Taking note of the need "to transform education so as to relate it to the life, need and aspirations of the people" the group of experts recommended, "Educational activity should be organized in such a way that always and ever, in each and every task, the child is encouraged to express and find its best fulfilment" (Framework, 1975, *passim*).

The recent National Policy on Education Resolution (1986) while noting that ". . . the general formulations incorporated in the 1968 Policy did not, however, get translated into a detailed strategy of implementation . . . ." It reiterated the same idea by stating, "Education refines sensitivities and perceptions that contribute to national cohesion, a scientific temper and independence of mind and spirit – thus furthering the goals of socialism, secularism and democracy enshrined in our Constitution" (NPE Resolution, 1986, p.3).

The National Curriculum for Elementary and Secondary Education (1988) which was placed before the CABE (1988) and received its approval, observed:

> Education is fundamental to all-round development-material and spiritual. Education is also viewed as an integral part of national development. Since the individual's capacity to contribute to national development is made possible and is enhanced by his or her development as an individual, one of the chief concerns of the curriculum at the school stage will have to be, to facilitate individual development and fulfilment.
>
> (Framework, Rev.Ver., 1988, p.7)

Thus, the various commissions and committees have not only emphasized the development of the individual but also need for this development to further the social goals of democracy, secularism and socialism. As pointed out by Malhotra, "It is only through a well designed and effectively implemented educational programme, the child could be equipped to realise his inner potential and to contribute meaningfully to national-building" (*supra* p.IV).

Learning and Cognitive Structure

Education has been referred to as an activity involving the teacher, the taught and the curriculum. The taught or the learner has a central position in the teaching learning process (Framework 1986, p.8), but the progress or efficiency of learning varies among students of more or less the same age and grade. This is so because students are not always ready, and equally ready, to engage successfully in learning tasks due to differences in their individual abilities. Understanding the individual differences among the students in terms of abilities is therefore, one of the primary tasks of educators. Bruner made a fervent plea for it by stating:

> Research on intellectual development of the child highlights the fact that at any stage of development the child has a characteristic way of viewing the world and explaining to himself. The task of teaching a subject to a child at any particular age is one of representing the structure of that subject in terms of the child's viewing the things.
>
> (Bruner, 1960, p.33)

Shulman while commenting upon the controversy regarding Science and Mathematics curriculum observed, "to identify whether the child is ready to learn a particular concept or principle, one analyzes the structure of what is to be taught and compares it, with what is already known about the cognitive structure of the child at that age", and suggested, "If they are consonant it can be taught, if they are dissonant it can not" (Shulman, 1968, p.190).

The Framework of Curriculum for the Ten Year School (1975) too while emphasizing "readiness is the foundation for learning", stated:

> The physical, intellectual and emotional levels of the child growth provides both the limiting conditions as also foundations of learning. A child is capable of acquiring much more . . . provided it is exposed to the right type of experience. This requires a very judicious planning and keen eye to identify the pupils' potentialities and inclination in order to provide suitable experience in line with his motivation and level of development.
>
> (Framework, 1975, p.33)

The National Curriculum for Primary and Secondary Education (1985) prepared by the NCERT after deliberations with various eminent educationists, curriculum specialist, subject experts etc., perceiving "the characteristics of learners at different stages of the intellectual development have implications for curriculum organization . . .", stated:

> Once the specific objectives under each of the area of study are formulated, they are required to be sequenced keeping in view not only their logical sequence but also the stages of intellectual development of the learner and the changes that take place as they move from the pre-primary to secondary stages.
>
> (Framework, 1986, pp.12-13, *passim*)

Subsequently, the revised version of this framework in order to make curriculum realistic, relevant and meaningful stated:

> The content and processes of education will have to be designed keeping in view the developmental needs of the pupil, his/her intellectual development and capability for learning at different stages of his/her development and the process and modes of his/her learning during these stages.
>
> (Framework Rev.Ver., 1988, pp.7-8)

Thus, for any kind of curriculum planning and innovation, the cognitive structure of the learners has to be taken into account. As far back as 1975, the Framework of Curriculum for the Ten Year School while identifying implications for implementation of new curriculum, suggested studies concerning motivation, learning, development and behavioural characteristics of children as one of the major areas of work (Framework, 1975, p.46). The Framework (1988) too recommended, "The minimum learning outcomes for each curricular areas will have to be specified keeping in view the research findings regarding the mental ability of pupils at different stages of their development" (Framework, 1988, p.13). Thus, there is a need to study the mental ability of the pupils at their different stages of development. For this purpose, a brief survey of ideas regarding the nature of mental ability or intelligence would be worthwhile.

Nature of Mental Ability

The concept of mental ability or intelligence is as old as history. The Chinese are said to be using intelligence and educational achievement tests to select civil servants as long back as in 2357 B.C. (Du Bois,

1970). The term 'intelligentia' is said to be coined by Roman Philosopher Cicero (Burt, 1955; Eysenck, 1979). However, the first discussion of the term mental ability appeared in the nineteenth century in the writings of a British scholar, Sir Francis Galton. Galton conceived that 'the only information that reaches us concerning outward events appears to pass through the avenues of our senses'. He therefore, proposed that intellectual features are dependent upon 'senses and physical-features'. In order to measure discriminating powers of sensory and physical faculties, Galton devised several ingenious tests, measuring instruments and a variety of schemes for obtaining data. Among his best known efforts was the establishment of an anthropometric laboratory for measurement of sensory discrimination, motor capacities, and other simple traits (Galton, 1883, *passim*). James McKeen Cattell in America was the first to introduce the term mental test. He also used Galton type of tests for predicting college grades and shared his view that an estimate of intellectual functioning could be obtained through tests of sensory discrimination and reaction time (Cattell, 1890). However, Ebbinghaus, who developed and used completion tests, sensed that complex test-tasks opened up the possibilities for estimation of higher mental processes. But, it was not until Binet and Simon who accepted the challenge thrown by educational authorities of Paris and Breslau to identify feeble-minded children, that something spectacular was attempted (Vernon, 1949).

The French psychologists, Binet and Simon sought to measure intelligence directly through the use of relatively complex tasks. In two articles published in 1905, Binet and Simon presented the original version of the now famous "Binet tests" (Anastasi, 1965, p.29). They described intelligence as a faculty consisting of judgement, otherwise called good sense, practical sense, initiative, the faculty of adopting one's self to circumstances. "To judge well, to comprehend well and to reason well" were the essential activities of intelligence according to them (Binet and Simon, 1905). Though Binet and Simon preferred such complex tests-tasks each of which were appropriate for analysis of a single ability but by adapting a single score for 'intelligence', they contradicted themselves (Guilford, 1967, p.12). This led Spearman to describe their thinking as 'inconceivably illogical' (Spearman, 1927, p.24).

Theoretical Definition

With the advent of tests to measure intelligence, psychologists felt the need to define it. It gave rise to various definitions, such as, "ability to learn" (Buckingham, p.273); "power of good responses from the point of view of truth or fact" (Thorndike, p.124); "ability of an individual to adapt himself adequately to relatively new situations in life" (Pinter, p.139); "capacity for knowledge and knowledge possessed" (Henmon, p.195); "capacity to acquire capacity" (Woodrow, p.207) etc., (Thorndike, *et al.*, 1921). These definitions reflected diversity of meanings and views. Nonetheless, systematic and relatively objective formulation of knowledge as essential characteristic of scientific psychology demanded definitions of intelligence that could satisfy the need of univocal communication in terms of observable and measurable operations, which resulted in a spade of operational definitions. However, a clue to the scientific solution of the problem was provided by Boring, who stated: "Intelligence as a measurable capacity must at the start be defined as the capacity to do well in an intelligence test" (Boring, 1923, pp.35-36). As a working definition, it pointed to the need for a careful study of tests themselves in terms of what they measure. Boring himself suggested, "We should be able to gain insight into the nature of tests through the method of correlation" (Guilford, 1967, p.13), which naturally implied inter-correlations among a set of tests as the first step towards factor analysis. This progressively led to the emergence of factor theories of intelligence ranging from Spearman's two factors theory to Guilford's arsenal of 120 distinct factors.

Two Factors Theory of Mental Ability

Spearman in Britain was the first who, by studying the correlations between tests of sensory discrimination (pitch, brightness, weight) and estimates of intelligence derived from school grades and ratings by teachers and classmates, could make a successful attempt to investigate the nature of mental functioning by empirical, quantitative methods. Thus, the seedling from which all else to clarify the nature of mental functioning through the method of factor analysis has sprung, lies in his theory. It was in 1904 that Spearman published his correlations between sensory tests and estimates of intelligence which showed that: 'all branches of intellectual activity have in common one fundamental function (or group of functions), whereas the remaining or specific elements of the activity seem in every case to be wholly different from that in all others'. Spearman's theory was eventually designated as two factor theory, since it analysed all intellectual functions into two classes of factors – a general (g) factor and specific (s) factors. It explained the tendency for all mental abilities to overlap to some extent and yet to show considerable unevenness. Spearman identified his 'g' factor as 'general mental energy' with which each individual is endowed and 's' factors as 'a large number of mechanisms or engines' which could be activated by this energy. He developed the 'tetrad differences' technique of proving that no significant factors other than 'g' and 's' are present (Vernon, *repr.* 1971, pp. 12-13 *passim*).

Thomson, however, conceived mental ability as comprising a large number of independent structural "bonds" including reflexes, habits, learned associations, and the like. According to him "Various kinds of behavioural tasks involved different samples of such bonds and the performance on a task activates a large number of these bonds. Thus the degree to which performance is correlated across tasks depend on the number of bonds that they have in common. The more the bonds they have in common that are sampled by the given tasks, the more highly they will be correlated, the correlation between the tests is a function of overlap between the sets of operations thus sampled" (Brown and Thomson, 1921). Thomson, thus, observed that the tasks are loaded on 'g' in proportion to the number of bonds they involve and the factor analysis of a set of tests will, therefore, given the appearance of a unitary general factor though the communality is not attributable to a unitary source of individual differences. This he called 'the theory of bonds'. Thomson thus did not agree with Spearman's psychological interpretation of a general factor without, however, questioning the validity of his mathematical discovery (Sternberg, 1985, p.20).

'g' plus Group Factors plus 's' Factors Theories

The chief criticism that arose against Spearman's two factor theory was that he failed to allow sufficiently for types of abilities which, less general than 'g', were certainly not specific. Though Spearman admitted that different number of tests show residual correlations over and above 'g', but he ascribed this to the presence of common specific factors and insisted that such 'specific overlap' was very rare. This led to the view that mental functioning in addition to 'g' and 's' involved certain other sets of abilities or group factors which are common to a few of the test and which themselves can be subdivided into numerous minor group factors. The chief proponent of this view were; Burt, Kelley, Stephenson, Koussy, Alexander and others. Burt (1909) obtained suggestive evidence of a sensory discrimination group factor beyond 'g' and later on provided evidence of verbal, numerical and practical group factors in school subjects in addition to a general factor. He also proposed Simple Summation technique of analysis which was subsequently used by Thurstone for his Centroid Method. Kelley (1928) too presented evidence for five group factors which he described as verbal, number, memory, spatial and speed factors in addition to a general factor. Stephenson (1931) provided evidence for a 'g' plus a verbal group factor and did not disprove the alternative of another group factor of a spatial-perceptual nature. Alexander (1935) in addition to 'g' found a v-factor, and a practical group factor which he called F. Blakey (1940) also found evidence for verbal, perceptual and spatial group factors in addition to 'g' (Vernon, *repr.* 1971, pp. 11-19 *passim*).

The widespread application of factor analysis during forties led to a rapid proliferation of factors. In an attempt to introduce order into this growing complexity, some psychologists proposed systematic schemes for the organization of intellectual factors. An arrangement that found fair acceptance particularly among British psychologists was called the hierarchical scheme first suggested by Burt (Anastasi, 1965, p. 65).

On the basis of previously identified factors. Burt (1949) dichotomized the human mind into intellectual and practical abilities. On the intellectual side of the human mind, he recognized in descending order (i) relations, (ii) associations, (iii) perceptions, and (iv) sensations. Under practical abilities he placed psychomotor, space and mechanical abilities and observed that practical abilities also vary in degree of generally at different levels like intellectual abilities and also the practical abilities of lower levels of generality bear subordinate relationships to those of higher levels. This hierarchical organization of mental factors, which Burt represented via the simile of inverted tree is shown in the Fig. 1.1.

Another British psychologist Vernon (1950) further elaborated the hierarchical scheme with special reference to factors of practical significance in educational and vocational guidance. He developed his model on the basis of factor analytic studies done on the samples of

Navy and Army recruits in Britain and likened his model to a branching hierarchy of a genealogical tree as illustrated in the Fig. 1.2.

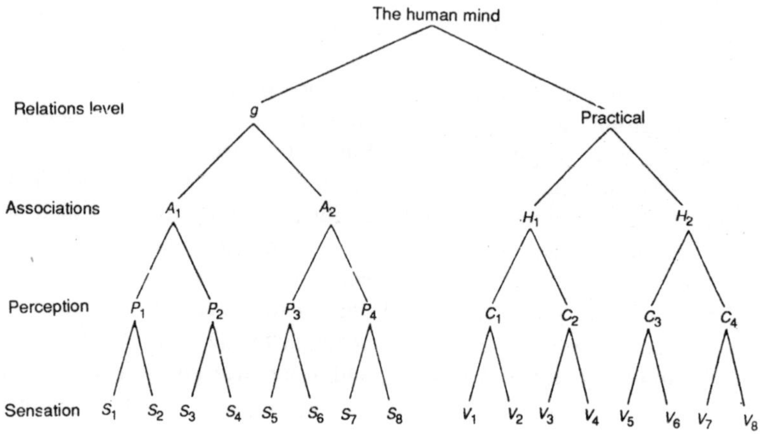

FIG. 1.1: Burt's Conception of the Organization of Mental Functioning

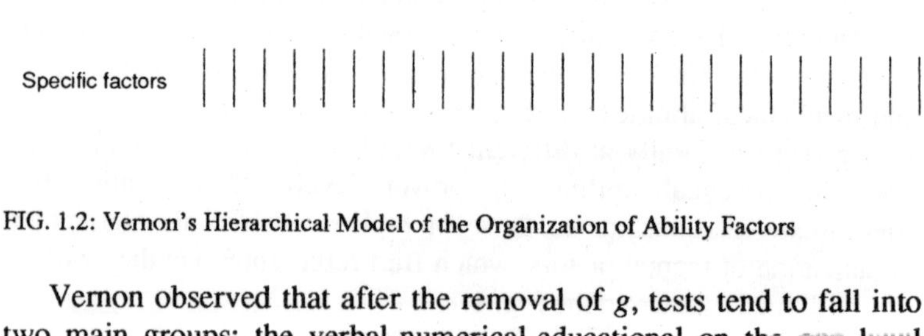

FIG. 1.2: Vernon's Hierarchical Model of the Organization of Ability Factors

Vernon observed that after the removal of *g*, tests tend to fall into two main groups: the verbal-numerical-educational on the one hand and the practical-mechanical-spatial-physical on the other hand. The former is referred to as the *v: ed* factor while the latter as the *k: m* factor. The *v: ed* factor further splits into verbal and numerical minor group factors. Similarly, *k: m* factor splits into mechanical information, spatial and manual sub-factors. Finally, minor group factors split into small factors specific to each test.

Multiple Factors Theories

Quite distinct from these view-points were the views of multiple factors theorists. The multiple factors theorists posited that intelligence is not a simple unitary trait or ability, nor has a hierarchical structure rather, it has many different and independent abilities. Thus, the view that a person receiving a high score on an "omnibus" test of intelligence is likely to be high or successful on all abilities tapped by that test and a person low on that test is likely to be doomed to failure, was an incorrect view. It was argued that a low score on a composite test of intelligence might conceal some particular kind of talent (Carroll, 1982). This brought into fore, the concept of differential ability factors. Two views, one by Thurstone and another by Guilford are – significant in this connection.

Thurstone (1938) after an analysis of fifty-six tests given to 240 college students by employing 'centroid method' identified nine factors: S-Space, P-Perceptual Speed, N-Number Facility, V-Verbal Relations, R-Memory, I-Induction W-Word Fluency, R-Restricted Reasoning and D-Deduction which he called basic or primary mental abilities. Thurstone's observation was different from that of British psychologists in the sense that there is not only one but many kinds of abilities and children with relatively low standing on general intelligence were not doomed to failure in everything of intellectual nature. These results revealed that people had a wide variety of strengths and weaknesses and they might differ in their abilities or aptitudes for different types of educational programmes, occupations and vocations (Thurstone, 1938, *passim*). Thus, Thurstone's theory of general structure of mind, represents the mind as containing a miscellaneous number of primary abilities, collected together with no definite or intelligible relations amongst or between them.

A significant development in the factorial analysis of intelligence or mental abilities came from the long range research by Guilford and his associates at the University of Southern California. On factor analyses of correlation matrices, Guilford (1959) conceived 120 factors which were sufficiently distinct by themselves. But he found that they could be classified in certain ways because they resemble one another.

According to Guilford, one way of classification of those factors was the basic kind of processes or operations performed. This classification gave him five major groups of intellectual abilities: factors of cognition (C), memory (M), convergent thinking (N), divergent thinking (D) and evaluation (E).

Cognition (C) to Guilford, was the first and basic kind of mental operation. Immediate discovery, awareness, rediscovery or recognition of particular items of information, comprehension or understanding were all instances of the operation of cognition. Memory (M) to him was fixation of information into memory storage, not to be confused with the memory store itself. Convergent production (N) was a kind of productive thinking which was concerned with the generation of information from the given information, where the needed information was fully determined by the given information. It was concerned with the search for logical imperatives or logic-tight deductions. Divergent production (D) was another kind of productive thinking which was concerned with the generation of logical alternatives from the given information, where the emphasis was upon variety, quantity and relevance of output from the same source. And finally evaluation (E) was the comparison of information with respect to given specifications in accordance with logical criteria such as identity, agreement and consistency; it was applied to the information that was cognized or retrieved from the memory storage in productive thinking.

A second way of classification of mental abilities, according to Guilford, was the kind of material or content involved, viz., figural (F), symbolic (S), semantic (M) and behavioural (B).

To Guilford, the figural (F) information was in the concrete form as perceived or recalled in the form of images through the sense of sight or hearing. The symbolic (S) information was in the form of denotative signs having no significance in and of themselves, such as letters, numbers and words. The semantic (M) information was in the form of meaning to which word commonly become attached. The meaningful pictures also conveyed semantic information to Guilford. And, finally, the behavioural (B) information to Guilford was involved in human interactions, where the attitudes, needs, desires, moods, intentions, perceptions, thoughts, etc., of different persons were involved.

A third way of classification of mental abilities, according to Guilford, was the products or the form taken by the information when a certain operation was applied to a certain kind of content. This gave him as many as six general kinds of product categories such as units

(U), classes (C), relations (R), systems (S), transformations (T) and implications (I).

The product units (U) to Guilford, were relatively segregated or circumscribed items of information which had "thing" character – might be close to Gestalt's 'figure on ground'. The product classes (C) were conceptions underlying sets of items of information grouped by virtue of their common properties. The product relations (R) were connections between items of information which were based upon variables or points of contact that applied to them. The product system (S) were complex items of information composed of more than two inter-connected units. The product transformation (T) were changes of various kinds – redefinition, revisions or modifications existed in the information or in its functions. And finally, implications (I) were the extrapolations of the information in the form of expectancies, predictions, or known or suspected consequences.

Guilford thus conceived intelligence as a collection of abilities for processing of information of various kinds in various way. The 120 distinct abilities which he posited in this way, were organized by him into a three dimensional model, calling it a 'morphological model of intellect', by means of a cuboid as given in Fig. 1.3.

Each cell of this cuboid thus represents one unique ability represented by a particular kind of mental operation applied to a particular type of content of information yielding a particular form or product of information. Guilford denoted this ability by a trigram symbol; the first letter of which represents the type of mental operation involved; the second type of content of information; and the third the form of the product of information.

Subsequently, Guilford (1977) bifurcated his content category of 'figural' into visual (V) and auditory (A) and thus instead of four content categories he had five content categories. This gave him 150 distinct mental factors, instead of 120 conceived by him earlier. This morphological model of human intellect has evolved from what is now called, Guilford's 'Structure of intellect theory'.

Factor Theories – Heterogeneity and Homogeneity of Selected Groups

The question of general, general plus group factors or multiple independent factors has also been examined by researchers from the angle of homogeneity or heterogeneity of the tested groups. Among the prominent studies in this context, was a study by Kelley (1928), which led him to observe that Spearman's '*g*' that was found in early factor analysis was due to the lack to homogeneity because of differences in age or maturity, race, nurture, sex, etc. Likewise, Thomson (1939) observed on the basis of re-analysis of his data that factor patterns are markedly affected by the heterogeneity or homogeneity of the group of persons tested. Equally important in this connection is Vernon's position when the stated, "The majority of American investigations were conducted on college students, aircraft pilots, high school pupils and other selected groups, because of which their results so readily fall into independent primary factors instead of '*g*' and group factors. But when more heterogeneous adult groups have been studies a '*g*' has usually appeared" (Vernon, *repr.*, 1971, p.31).

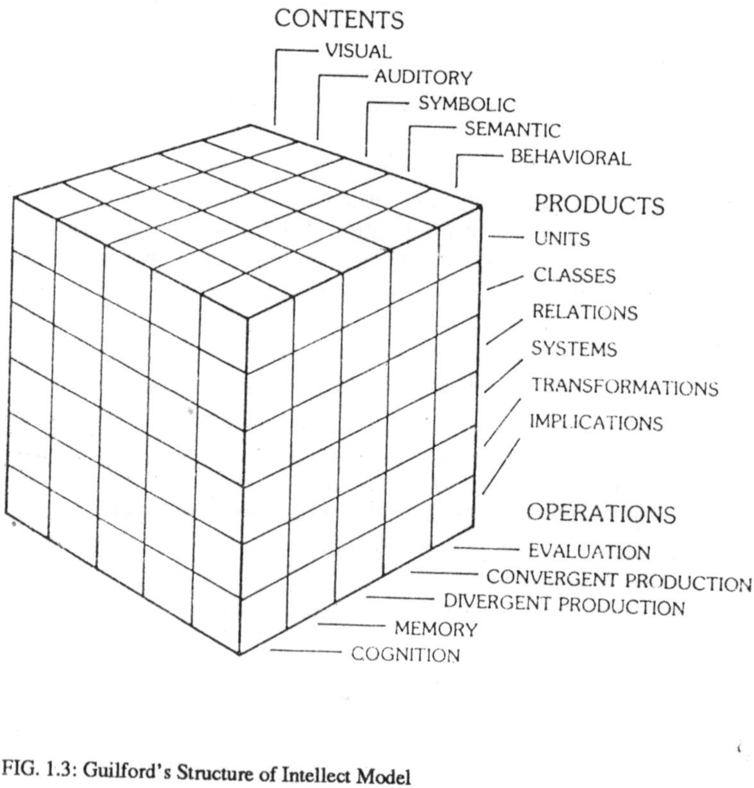

FIG. 1.3: Guilford's Structure of Intellect Model

Thurstone (1945) was however of the view, "Selection does distort the sizes of the factor loadings, but not the main factor pattern...". Vernon commenting on this stated, "In most investigation of college students, selection is based on a great variety of socio-economic, educational and other influences which are likely to be correlated with any factor other than '*g*'. Hence '*g*' variance only is reduced and no harm is done" (Vernon, *op.cit* p.131). Guilford, *et al.*, in a series of research with high grade groups, such as, airforce pilots and university students arrived at the conclusion that numerous intellectual factors can be distinguished in the fields of reasoning, planning, judgement, originality, etc., and that it would be profitable to develop tests for these, than for a vaguely conceived general capacity of intelligence.

While substantiating his own view, Vernon indirectly supported Thurston's and Guilford's position. By using group factor technique he found a '*g*' (with some twenty two per cent variance) + group factor for verbal, mechanical and spatial perceptual tests (totalling some twelve percent), which gave almost as good fit as Guilford's six multiple factors: Verbal, Mechanical, Visualization, General Reasoning, Reasoning II, and Judgement (Vernon, *repr.* 1971, p.56). However, Vernon used the evidence to posit that analysis of selected groups, like, that of Thurstone and Guilford are useful for bringing up group factors which might otherwise be obscured.

Thus, the question of '*g*', '*g*' plus group factors or multiple independent factors of mental ability still remains open till an attempt is made to study the nature of individual differences in mental ability with the help of data gathered from a particular social context for groups which can be identified as heterogeneous and homogeneous on the basis of a reasonable criterion.

Factor Theories – Differentiation of Mental Ability

Another issue which has bearing on organization of mental abilities or their pattern concerns differentiation of mental abilities. On the basis of studies undertaken earlier, Garrett observed, "Abstract or symbol intelligence changes in its organization as age increases from a fairly unified and general ability to a loosely organized group of abilities" (Garrett, 1946). If this is so, the pattern of mental abilities may not be clearly demarked, till each ability matures. Again, as stated by Garrett, "Over the elementary school years, we find a functional generality among tests at the symbolic level. Later on this general factor or '*g*' breaks down into the quasi-independent factors reported by many investigators" (Anastasi, 1965, p.80). This assertion was perhaps made to bring about a rapproachment between different theories of mental ability. However, for the ability factors to be clearly distinguishable, it needs to be known as to when the general factor, or '*g*' breaks down into the quasi-independent factors. Anastasi (1936), however, after summarizing a large number of investigations was of the opinion, ". . . though there are strong indications of alternations in factor patterns with age and training, the evidence for differentiation is far from unanimous" (Vernon, *repr.* 1971, p.29). Thus both the view required finding out the age at which factor patterns are properly distinguishable and hopefully are more or less stable.

Efforts have been made in the past to find out the age or period at which various mental abilities emerge and could be measured. Slater (1943) on administration of tests designed to measure '*g*', '*v*' and '*k*' to groups of 11 plus children, 13 plus children and 18 plus trade apprentices concluded that paper pencil tests of spatial judgement do not show any differentiation of spatial abilities among children before the age of 14 at least. Dempster (1947) on administration of four tests of verbal nature, four spatial tests and two general ability tests to boys between the age of $11^1/_2$ and $13^1/_2$ at six monthly intervals posited, "The abilities associated with verbal and spatial work seem to be maturing at comparable speeds during these years" (Dempster, 1948, p. 125). Edward on the basis of available empirical evidence observed, "Certain special abilities are more apparent and can be measured more easily after 13" (Edward, 1960, p.62).

A major attempt for examining the question of maturation, and by implication of differentiation of abilities, was made by Thurstone. He derived curves for each of his seven primary mental abilities after administration of his PMA tests to a large numbers of Chicago school students of ages five through seventeen. On extrapolation of his growth curves to the time of birth at the one extreme and to the age of nineteen at the other, and by comparing the curve on the basis of the age at which the average child reaches 80 per cent of maturity, he was able to estimate the age of 12 years for Perceptual Speed (P); age of 14 years for Space (S); age of 14 years for Reasoning (R); age of 16 years for Memory (M); age of 16 years for Number Facility (N); age of 18 years for Verbal Comprehension (V); later than 20 years for World Fluency (W) (Guilford, 1967, p. 420).

Thus, for the identification of the pattern of mental abilities one has not only to decide which ability or a class of abilities to choose but also to decide the age or stage. Together with this, if data can be gathered for a heterogeneous and a homogeneous group belonging to a particular social context then a relatively differentiated pattern can be identified, and its relationship with scholastic achievement variables can be deciphered for planning of curriculum and innovations in instructional strategies.

In view of the available empirical evidence, it appeared that one of the significant abilities for scholastic achievement especially in the area of Science and Mathematics which have been much emphasized in the new curriculum framework (1988) and has been investigated here, happens to be 'reasoning' (Bala, 1977; Chhikara, 1982; Tewari, 1985; Singh, 1987; Tyagi, 1987). Also reasoning ability has been a part of the intelligence tests from the inception of the testing movement. Some of the best known tests of intelligence, such as, the Miller Analogies Test, Raven's Progressive Matrices, Cattell's Culture Fair Test of *g* etc., involve reasoning test-tasks in one form or another. Those who participated in the symposium on the concept of intelligence, *Journal of Educational Psychology*, (vol. 12, 1921), also emphasized in one way or the other, intelligence in terms of reasoning (Sternberg, 1982, p.225). Not is this all. In almost all the major psychometric theories of intelligence reasoning has been considered to be a major component. The earliest factor analyst, Spearman (1904) said that the two sources of mental functioning, i.e., "eduction of relations' and 'eduction of correlates', which are involved in '*g*' are certainly component of 'reasoning'. Likewise, in Thurstone's (1938) theory of Primary Mental Abilities, 'reasoning' was one of the seven primary mental abilities. Guilford's theory of the Structure-of-Intellect (SOI) also drawn heavily upon reasoning operations (Sternberg, *op.cit.* p.226). Thus, whatever be the nature of mental ability or abilities, 'reasoning' has been one the most significant components. The author, therefore, decided to carry out a study on the pattern of reasoning abilities. Further, considering the studies by Thurstone, Edward, and others, it appeared that 14+ level holds good promise for a fruitful study into the pattern of reasoning ability. However, before carrying out such a study, it would be worthwhile at this stage to understand the concept of 'reasoning'.

The Concept of Reasoning

The origin of the concept of 'reasoning' as a method to arrive at truth dates back to early Greek civilization. It had its roots in the work of Ionian philosophers who, instead of explaining away observed phenomenon with a 'word' or 'words' (hypostastisation), insisted upon suggesting a 'hypothesis' about the phenomenon to arrive at truth. Subsequently, Socrates evolved his dialectical method. The Greek mathematicians including Pythagoras evolved the deductive method. Though Pythagoras is also credited with experimentation as a method to test the hypothesis, but his preference for deductive method led him to insisted upon maintaining a hypothesis even it was not substantiated by experimentation. It was left to Archimedes to reinstate the primacy of 'experimentation' for 'induction' and give some shape to 'scientific method' of reasoning, or to the inductive method. However, the work of Aristotle on formal logic, especially his method of syllogistic reasoning, did not let inductive method to flower till the end of dark-age and beginning of middle-age.

During the modern period, reasoning has been viewed in 'various way'. Dewey (1899) has treated it almost as being synonymous with problem solving in which a person reasons out the solution of a problem in a systematic fashion, often making use of logical principles and relevant past experiences. He uses all his experiences relevant to the problems together to try-out various combinations until he arrives at the correct solution. Even those, who do not follow Dewey, agree that reasoning does not occur until a problem or a difficulty is felt which cannot be solved by mere repetitions of earlier solutions, or by overt trial and error, and for which there is no ready answer. To Burt 'reasoning' is an activity, the results of which are expressed by arguments made up of series of propositions or sentences logically connected (Burt, 1949, pp. 110 & 111). To Garrett, reasoning is thinking with a purpose or goal in which use is made of past experiences and in which organization and logical arrangement of responses is demanded (Garrett, 1955, pp. 414-418). To others, reasoning is a process of controlled thinking or association which starts with some problem of interest to the reasoner and directed towards its solution (Ellis, 1965, p.219). To Sternberg, it is an attempt to combine elements of old information to form new information (Sternberg, 1982, p.235).

Be that as it may, two major forms of reasoning, induction and deduction have been of major concern among philosophers and psychologists during the last and early part of present century. The term 'induction' signifies reasoning from particular to general whereas 'deduction' signifies reasoning from general to the particular, or more specifically from stated premises to a particular conclusion. Obviously, various efforts have been made from time to time to elaborate the concept of reasoning or induction and deduction. It may be interesting at this stage to review the relevant studies and literature, specifically touching upon psychometric studies on reasoning, a resume of which follows in the next chapter.

2

REASONING: A Research Framework

WITH THE emergence of modern scientific psychology, the domain of reasoning has been variously defined. Apart from the *a priori* postulations, some significant theoretical postulations based on empirical referents were made by innovative use of factor analytic procedures. In America, the investigation by Thurstone (1938) was perhaps the first major attempt which helped him to identify three reasoning factors: Induction (I), Restricted Reasoning (R) and Deduction (D) by adopting his own 'centroid method' of factor analysis. The tests which emerged with significant loadings on Thurstone's Induction factor (I) were: Number Series, Tabular Completion, Areas, Figure Classification and Pattern Analogies. The characteristic common to all these tests was that they all required the subjects 'to find out a rule or a principle in each item'. The tests which had significant loadings on his Restricted Reasoning factor (R) were: Arithmetical Reasoning, Vocabulary (Thorndike), Numerical Judgement, Completion, Vocabulary (Chicago) and Mechanical Movements. The characteristic common to all these tests was posited by Thurstone tentatively as 'successful completion of a task that involves some form of restriction in the solution'. The tests which had significant loadings on his Deduction factor (D) were: False Premises, Reasoning, Mechanical Movements and Figure Classification. Thurstone did not find this list of tests sufficiently extensive to make the identification of his Deduction factor (D) with certainty. But the obvious common feature in most of the test-tasks of the above four tests was 'deduction' (Thurstone, 1938, pp. 86-89).

Studies Focusing on Traditional Concepts of Reasoning

The model age of the subjects of Thurstone's (1938) study was eighteen years and they were a highly selected group (*supra*, pp. 16-17). However, in younger groups Induction (I), Deduction (D) and

Restricted Reasoning (R) factors appeared to amalgamate as Thurstone and Thurstone (1941) in an analysis of sixty tests given to 710 pupils aged around fourteen years found only one reasoning factor – Induction which was given a better name Reasoning by them (Vernon, *repr.* 1971, p.20). Thurstone's followers, such as, Davidson (1945), Taylor (1947), Fruchter (1948) and others also found only one Reasoning factor in younger groups.

In some researches, Thurstone's R or 'reasoning to a limited solution' was found amalgamated with D-deduction, or 'reasoning from general to the specific'; in others with I-induction or 'finding out the underlying principle'. For instance, Blaskey (1941) on an analysis of a battery of eleven reasoning tests identified two distinct factors: Induction and Deduction. Also Botzum (1951) on an analysis of forty-six tests administered to 237 college men confirmed two distinct reasoning factors: Induction and Deduction. The leading test for Botzum's Induction factor were: Letter Series, Number Series, Numerical Judgement and Verbal Analogies, and his Deduction factor was marked by False Premises, Figure Classification, Reasoning I and Figure Grouping.

Zimmerman (1953) after re-analysis of Thurstone's entire PMA battery agreed with Thurstone regarding his Deduction factor but did not find evidence for his Induction factor. Possibly, in partial replacement, he found a factor which he called Eduction of Relationship (ER). Still another factor, Reasoning (R) which did not emerge in a well defined manner in Thurstone's investigation, was identified by Zimmerman who called at General Reasoning (GR). The common test that linked the two, was Arithmetical Reasoning – an unfailing type of marker test (Guilford & Hoepfner, 1971, p.9).

Butt (1957) analysed twenty-three tests among 200 thirteen to fourteen-year old boys and girls of around average ability. He obtained a clear-cut Induction group factor in Number and Letter Series, Abstraction, Concept Formation and Matrices; also a Deduction factor in Syllogisms, Pedigree, Reasoning Problems, Coding and Arithmetical Problems (Vernon, *op cit.*, p. 155).

In an early research carried out under Burt which was later on described by Wheeler (1958), verbal intelligence was held constant. The main factor in a long series of verbal and practical reasoning problem tests was defined as organizing data into logically coherent systems. This sub-divided into minor group factors – analytic or explicit and synthetic or implicit, which clearly corresponded to the so-called deductive and inductive type. An additional factor running through many but not all of the tests was called Apprehension of Relations but its function in reasoning was not made clear (Wheeler, 1958, pp.137-159).

These studies focused by and large on traditional concepts of reasoning as induction and/or deduction, besides some other aspects proposed by logicians. Some of the more recent studies like that of Dorminey (1972), Cox (1972), Barlow (1974), Noble (1974), Munoz (1977), Ross (1977), Northrop (1977), Sternberg (1978), Evans (1978), Eritsyan (1980), Daniel (1982), Duroy (1986) etc., also focus upon inductive and/or deductive processes and skills of reasoning in on way or the other.

Alternative Interpretations

Certain studies undertaken during and after Second World War broke away from the traditional concepts of induction and deduction. For instance, Guilford and Lacey (1947) in a number of analyses performed by Guilford and his collaborators during Second World War in the U.S. Army Air Force Aviation Psychology Research programme, in the area of reasoning, identified three factors: Reasoning-I, Reasoning-II and Reasoning-III. Reasoning-I was marked by arithmetical reasoning tests consistently. It was called "general reasoning" since a number of other tests varying widely in nature had common loadings on it. Thurstone (1938) probably had much of the same factor for which his Arithmetical Reasoning Test was highest in the list. Reasoning-II was conspicuously marked by a Figure Analogies Test – suggesting that the factor involved seeing relations. Correspondence of this factor to Thurstone's Induction (I) factor was considered doubtful as the latter was more complex than seeing merely 'relations'. Reasoning-III was marked by two tests, one called Spatial Reasoning and another Decoding. The former required the discovery of a principle that applied to the placement of letters X and Y in a series of dashes while latter required the deciphering of a code by which letters in words are associated with flags. Hence, Reasoning-III appeared closer to Thurstone's Induction factor I). The results of these analyses revealed nothing that could be related to Thurstone's Deduction factor (D) (Guilford & Hoepfner, 1971, pp.62-63).

Rimoldi (1951), in an attempt to establish a '*g*' factor in the second order domain, administered a battery of twenty-five reasoning tests to

384 children between the ages of eleven and fourteen years studying in twelve schools in a city of Argentina. On factor analyzing the correlation matrix by Thurstone's centroid method he identified the following seven primary factors:

I. Bringing Together of Several Conflicting Gestalts (Plasticity)
II. Not interpreted (but possibly number)
III. Finding Relationship
IV. Finding Likeness
V. Eduction of Correlates
VI. Verbality
VII. Globalization (bringing parts together for a solution)

The second order analysis gave him three factors, Factor-A, Factor-B and Factor-C. Factor-A was identified as 'finding likeness' because it had highest loading on primary factor, Factor-IV, and lowest loading on primary factors, Factor-I, Factor-III and Factor-V. Factor-B was interpreted as referring to the 'mechanisms involved in dealing with relations, the education of correlates and globalization' as it had its highest loadings for primary factors, Factor-III, Factor-V and Factor-VII. The loadings of the primary factors, Factor-I, Factor-II, Factor-VI and Factor-VII on Factor-C indicated that it represented 'synthetic process' (Rimoldi, 1951, pp.75-101).

A large scale research of Adkins and Lyerly (1952) was designed to elucidate the nature of reasoning among army personnel. They administered a battery of sixty-five tests intended to measure reasoning and reference factors to a representative sample of 226 army men in the age group from twenty-three to twenty-eight years. The men were so selected that the distribution of their scores on Army Classification Battery's aptitude areas covered a wide range. Product-moment correlation coefficients were worked out after normalizing the scores. On factor analysis of the correlation matrix by centroid method and then rotating the centroid orthogonal reference frame to a oblique structure, sixteen factors were identified. Only five of these sixteen factors were related to reasoning namely:

I. Flexibility of Perceptual Closures
II. Hypothesis Verification
III. Perception of Abstract Similarities
IV. Concept Formation
V. Deduction

Factor-I had its highest loadings for two figure classification tests: Map Planning, and Camouflaged Outlines and Decoding. Factor-II had its highest loadings for Progressive Matrices sub-tests, Practical Situations, Series (figural), Logical Puzzle and Word Selection. Factor-III was concerned with educing relations of similarity, but as the quality of flexibility in many tests loaded on it, apparently outweighted the importance of educing relations of similarity, it was identified as 'Perception of Abstract Similarities'. This factor had its highest loading on two verbal classification and two analogies tests. Factor-IV had loadings for Picture Group Naming, Verbal Analogies, Word Group Naming and Matrices. Factor-II, Factor-III & Factor-IV represented components of the factor described by Thurstone and others as Induction. Factor-V had its highest loading for False Premises Test and Identical Forms Test. This factor agreed well with the factor Thurstone and other investigators had called 'Deduction'. The study did not confirm Thurstone's Restricted Reasoning Factor (Adkins and Lyerly, 1952, *passim*).

ARP Studies on Reasoning

A significant contribution to the description of the domain of reasoning was made by Guilford and his associates at the University of Southern California under Aptitude Research Project (ARP). While starting from the list of factors identified in the US Army Air Force Studies, Guilford and his associates at the University of Southern California, were particularly concerned with the variety and structure of higher intellectual abilities, claiming with good justification that these are too diverse and complex to be represented by a single factor. Guided by results of previous factor analytic studies and a theoretical analysis of some domains of intellect, they began their study of that domain by postulating a set of hypothetical components or distinct abilities. They constructed several tests to cover each of those components and administered them to the military subjects of the same sex who were already earmarked for officer status, and whose average IQ was moderately high and range of IQs was somewhat limited (Guilford & Hoepfner, 1971, p.14). Two studies under this project were specifically conducted to investigate the domain of reasoning. These were listed by Guilford and Hoepfner (1971) as Reasoning-A and Reasoning-B analyses. One study under this project was undertaken to clarify 'general reasoning'. A study on 'reasoning' along with the domains of 'creativity' and 'evaluation' was also undertaken under this project. The age range of the subjects of these studies was approximately eighteen to twenty-five years.

Reasoning-A Analysis

Green, *et al.*, (1953) attempted to isolate and define the primary factors in the domain of reasoning by setting up four hypotheses and various sub-hypotheses under each as suggested by Guilford and Lacey (1947) and Thurstone (1938) studies. Their test battery consisted of twenty eight reasoning tests pertaining to those hypotheses and six tests which defined non-reasoning factors. The battery was administered to a sample of 144 Air Force Officer candidates and 139 cadets. On factor analysis of the correlation matrix by Thurstone's complete centroid method and rotating the axes by Zimmerman's orthogonal rotation method, thirteen orthogonal factors were identified. Seven of them were reasoning factors, namely:

I. General Reasoning (GR)
II. Logical Reasoning (LR)
III. Eduction of Perceptual Relations (PR)
IV. Eduction of Conceptual Relations (CR)
V. Eduction of Conceptual Patterns (CP)
VI. Eduction of Correlates (EC)
VII. Symbol Substitution (SS)

Most of the test that appeared on General Reasoning factor (Factor-I), involved manipulation of abstract symbols that had little realistic meaning. However, as problems get harder trial-and-error manipulation may reasonably be assumed to become more important. This factor, therefore, represented a less logical manipulation of symbols in a trial-and-error fashion. It corresponded to Thurstone's Restrictive Reasoning and Army Air Force Reasoning-I. On Logical Reasoning factor (Factor-II) strictly logical and syllogistic type of tests were conspicuously loaded, and it appeared like the factor that was identified Deduction (D) by Thurstone and other investigators. Guilford and Hoepfner (1971) called it Logical Reasoning because it appeared to them as an ability to evaluate inference – not the ability involved in drawing conclusions. Eduction of Perceptual Relations (Factor-III), Eduction of Conceptual Relations (Factor-VI) and

Eduction of Conceptual Patterns (Factor-V) could be regarded as Thurstone's Induction (I) or three different component of it. Eduction of Correlates (Factor-VI) was close to what could be called Deduction (D), but it was a somewhat special case of 'deduction' found in reasoning by analogy. Symbol Substitution (Factor-VII) had no parallel in previous findings. The most notable outcome of this study was that to the question, though of more general nature, viz., whether there is distinction between concrete (Eduction of Perceptual Relations) and abstract (Eduction of Conceptual Relations) reasoning, it provided an answer.

Reasoning-B Analysis

Guilford, *et al.*, (1954) administered a batter of fifty-four tests which consisted of twenty-seven tests from Reasoning-A analysis, twenty-two tests from Air Force battery and five new tests, to 395 air force cadets and 343 student officers. The total sample included six samples of air cadets, four samples of student officers and five mixed samples. The groups were comparable with respect to age and education as nearly all examines were in their early twenties and had some college education. However, the comparison of test score means of various groups yielded significant differences. These differences indicated that the fifteen groups did not represent a homogeneous population with respect to what the tests measure. To the extent that this bias introduced correlations between means of the test scores, and thus spuriousness into the correlations between means of the test scores, the score distribution were dichotomized near the median in case of each test for each group in order to remove this spurious component in correlations. Tetrachoric correlation coefficients were computed on the basis of these dichotomized score distributions. As the correlations between means represented genuine differences in ability, this procedure led to loss of some true-variances. However, it provided some form of adjustment in the means and dispersions of the score distributions by equalizing them approximately. On factor analysis of the correlation matrix by Hotelling's principal component method and then rotating the axes by Zimmerman's graphic orthogonal rotation method, sixteen factors were extracted. Of these, only five were in the area of reasoning, namely:

I. General Reasoning (GR)

II. Logical Reasoning (LR)
III. Eduction of Correlates (EC)
IV. Eduction of Conceptual Relations (CR)
V. Eduction of Perceptual Relations (PR)

Of the three tests that were found to have significant loading on General Reasoning factor (Factor-I) in Reasoning-A analysis, two, i.e., Ship Destination Test and Letter Triangle Test had marked loadings on Factor-I in this analysis also. Arithmetic Reasoning, a problem solving test led the list in both the analyses. Thus, General Reasoning factor was considered a well established factor. The leading tests for Logical Reasoning factor (Factor-II) in this analysis and in Reasoning-A analysis also, were of somewhat formal syllogistic type. The feature common to these tests appeared to be application of rules instead of furnishing deductions. Therefore, Logical Reasoning factor (Factor-II) was different from Deduction (D). Investigators preferred to classify it as an evaluative ability. The leading test (Correlate Completion) for Education of Correlates factor (Factor-III) in both Reasoning-A and Reasoning-B analyses was of completion type, and in Reasoning-A analysis Figure Analogies Completion Test was strong. Eduction of Correlates factor was, therefore, described as 'the finding of proper words or figures to complete a relationship that has been given or recognized'. This factor was related to Air Force Reasoning-III. Eduction of Conceptual Relations factor (Factor-IV) emerged in Reasoning-A analysis also with Verbal Analogies-I leading the list of tests. It was similar to Perception of Abstract Similarities factor identified in Adkins and Lyerly's (1952) study. No factor comparable to this, emerged in Air Force Research. The interpretation of Eduction of Perceptual Relations factor (Factor-V) was more definite as all the three perceptual tests had their highest loading on it. It emerged in Reasoning-A analysis also. A somewhat similar factor, Reasoning-II emerged in Air Force Research also.

The Reasoning-B analysis thus supported the findings of Reasoning-A analysis that at least two reasoning factors were involved in 'Eduction of Relations'. These two factors stood in contrast to the nature of the three other reasoning factors found in this analysis, which did not appear to transcend the perceptual-conceptual dichotomy.

The Study of General Reasoning

This study was designed by Kettner, *et al.*, (1956) to make a concentrated analysis of a factor that has been relatively easy to isolate and cross-identify in factor-analytic studies but which was difficult to define. Of the many characteristics that were suggested common to the tests correlated with General Reasoning factor, three of the most plausible were selected for special attention. These were: Defining Problems, Handling Complicated Procedures, and Trial-and-Error Manipulation. A battery of twenty-three tests covering these hypotheses and five reference factors, was administered to an entering class of U.S. Coast Guard Academy cadets, 170 in number. On factor analysis of the correlation coefficients between the raw scores on these tests by Thurstone's complete centroid method and then rotating the axes by Zimmerman's graphic orthogonal method, ten factors were extracted. Of these ten, only three factors were of special interest in relation to the experimental tests representing three hypotheses of 'general reasoning'. These were:

I. General Reasoning (GR)
II. Handling Complicated Procedures (HCP)
III. Trial-and-Error Manipulation (TEM)

Of all the tests, three arithmetic-reasoning type of tests, Ship Destination, Necessary Arithmetic Operations and Necessary Facts which stressed the early stages of solving arithmetic-reasoning problems, had their highest loading on General Reasoning factor (Factor-I). Two other tests which were concerned with an early as well as late stages in achieving problem solutions, had secondary loadings on this factor and it was posited that General Reasoning factor had something to do with 'comprehending or structuring problems in preparation for solving them or the ability to structure problems'. Handling Complicated Procedures and Trial-and-Error Manipulation factors (Factor-II and Factor-III) were found to be distinct from General Reasoning factor.

Study of Reasoning, Creativity and Evaluation

Kettner, *et al*., (1959) conducted a study to investigate in the same analysis the domain of reasoning, creativity and evaluation. Fifty-seven tests, of which forty belonged to the domain of reasoning, were used in this study. The entire battery was broken into three partially overlapping batteries. Each battery was administered to a sample of approximately 200 air cadets who were typically in their early 20's, above the average as to their general intelligence, and had education of the level of high-school graduation or beyond. Pearson's product moment correlations were computed between the tests for the three batteries. These were then factor analyzed using Thurstone's complete centroid method. On rotating the axes by Zimmerman's graphic orthogonal method, following factors in the domain of reasoning were identified:

I. General Reasoning (GR)
II. Eduction of Perceptual Relations (PR)
III. Perceptual Classification (PC)
IV. Eduction of Conceptual Relations (CR)
V. Verbal Classification (VC)
VI. Eduction of Patterns (EP)
VII. Eduction of Correlates (EC)
VIII. Eduction of Structural Relations (SR)
IX. Symbol Manipulation (SM)
X. Symbol Substitution (SS)
XI. Naming Abstractions (NA)
XII. Eduction of Conceptual Correlates (CC)

As earlier, General Reasoning factor (Factor-I) was defined as the ability to comprehend or to structure problems in preparation for solving them. Eduction of Perceptual Relations factor (Factor-II) was defined as the ability to see perceptual relations as all the tests which had significant loadings on it, involved seeing relations in the figural material. In Reasoning-A and Reasoning-B analyses, the list of tests for Eduction of Perceptual Relations factor had contained tests in which seeing similarities seemed to be the main feature alongwith tests in which relations seemed to be the main feature. However, in the present study, the tests which had their main feature seeing similarities were separated from those concerned with seeing relations. They appeared together on a Perceptual Classification factor (Factor-III). The tests loaded significantly on Eduction of Conceptual Relations factor (Factor-IV) and Verbal Classification factor (Factor-V) involved seeing relations and similarities in the conceptual material respectively. A factor similar to Eduction of Patterns (Factor-VI) was identified in Reasoning-A analysis also. There it was called Eduction of Conceptual Patterns and defined as the ability to see rules, principles, or systems.

But in the present analysis, all the tests which had significantly loading on Eduction of Patterns factor were structural (symbolic) in material, so it could have been called Eduction of Structural Relations factor. However, the investigators simply called it, 'Eduction of Patterns', pending new empirical evidence. The tests significantly loaded on Eduction of Correlates factor (Factor-VII) stressed 'producing something to fit a given relation' and they were both figural as well as structural. Since all but one of the tests significantly loaded on Eduction of Structural Relations factor (Factor-VIII) were composed of letters and since most tests involved seeing relations, it was recognized as third relations seeing factor. Identification of this factor led to the possibility of finding a classification factor involving structural material as both a perceptual-classification and verbal classification factors were already recognized. Symbol Manipulation factor (Factor-IX) was the same as Handling Complicated Procedures factor found in General Reasoning Study (Kettner, *et al.*, 1956). Symbol Substitution factor (Factor-X) was defined as the ability to substitute symbols quickly. It differed from the preceding one in that no trial-and-error manipulation seemed to be necessary. The tests significantly loaded on Naming Abstractions factor (Factor-XI) called for naming of classes, relations, or trends. It was similar to one found by Adkins and Lyerly (1951), which they called Concept Formation. However, Naming Abstractions factor as emerged in the present study was more restricted; because all the tests (except Picture-Group Naming) loaded significantly on it were verbal, whereas Concept Formation included perceptual, structural as well as verbal tests. The tests significantly loaded on Eduction of Conceptual Correlates factor (Factor-XII) involved finding something to fit a given conceptual relation.

The results of this study led to believe that there was a group of factors which represented abilities to classify objects separate from the group of abilities to cognize relations; and there appeared to be as many as three in each group, having to do with figural, structural and verbal material respectively. It gave impetus to the attempts to organize the intellectual factors in a morphological system called "Structure of Intellect" (Guilford, 1956; 1957; 1958).

A trend which was discernible in all these ARP studies and all those which were concerned with the alternative interpretations of reasoning was to describe the concept in terms of more and more independent factors conceptualized on the basis of the tasks involved in various tests of reasoning. Thus, these studies emphasized finer and finer description of the concept in terms of empirical referents. Another significant feature of all these studies had been that these were conducted on selected group of army or navy recruits who were above average in IQ and were above 17+.

Targeted Rotations of ARP Studies on Reasoning

With the development of Cliff's (1966) method of rotation of congruency of factor matrices, all the earlier Aptitude Research Project Studies were re-done with an over-riding concern to achieve invariance of psychological factors. The results substantiated Guilford's Structure-Of-Intellect (SOI) theory.

In the targeted rotation of Reasoning-A data, Figure Exclusion Test and Figure Classification Test helped to identify a factor Cognition of Figural Classes (CFC). Circle Reasoning Test, Letter Triangle Test and Secret Writing Test led to the identification of a factor Cognition of Symbolic Systems (CSS). The tests involving relations between or amongst verbal concepts emerged together to identify a factor Cognition of Semantic Relations (CMR). Problem Solving Test, Ship Destination Test and Essential Operations Tests helped to determine the factor Cognition of Semantic Systems (CMS), providing much sharper picture of the factor General Reasoning. Form Reasoning Test and Secret Writing Test emerged together to represent a factor Convergent Production of Symbolic Implications (NSI). Syllogisms Test, Inference Test and False Premises Test which appeared together on Logical Reasoning factor in the original analysis, got differentiated in the targeted analysis. As relations were evaluated in these (syllogistic) tests, these divided their loadings between Evaluation of Semantic Relations (EMR) and Evaluation of Semantic Implications (EMI) (Guilford and Hoepfner, 1971, pp.73-90).

The targeted solution for Reasoning-B data agreed well with the targeted solution for Reasoning-A data. Figure Classification Test and Figure Exclusion Test again identified Cognition of Figural Classes (CFC). Mechanical Principles Test (an Air Force Test) together with Punched Holes Test emerged on a factor Cognition of Figural Transformations (CFT). Letter Triangle Test and Circle Reasoning Test again helped to identify Cognition of Symbolic Systems (CSS). Word Classification Test emerged as a signlet to identify Cognition of Semantic Classes (CMC). Cognition of Semantic Relations (CMR) did not require any other factor to account for the hypothesis 'seeing identity of relations' as Identical Verbal Relations Test was very strongly loaded on it. The lone concept to describe the general reasoning factor: Cognition of Semantic Systems (CMS) appeared to require 'understanding of the problem structure semantically', as Essential Operations Test along with Reading Comprehension Test had highest loading on it. Word Group Naming Test together with Naming Trends Test emerged on the naming factor: Convergent Production of Semantic Units (CMU). The two Number Operation Changes tests, which helped to determine Evaluation of Symbolic Relations (ESR) in Reasoning-A re-analysis, showed lack of invariance Test emerged on a factor Convergent Production of Symbolic Implications (NSI). Inference Test and Syllogisms Test together emerged on the factor Evaluation of Semantic Implications (EMI). False Premises Test was not included in Reasoning-B analysis. Absurdities Test got separated from Evaluation of Semantic Implication (EMI) tests (*supra.* pp.92-93).

In the targeted solution for General Reasoning Study, Secret Writing Test and Circle Reasoning Test along with Rules Test emerged on the factor Cognition of Symbolic Systems (CSS). Cognition of Semantic Systems (CMS) factor which was identified 'general reasoning' earlier, was identified by Ship Destination Test, Necessary Facts Test, Essential Operations Test, Necessary Arithmetic Operations Test, Circle Square Triangle Test and Balances Test, Problem Solving Test and Arithmetic Reasoning Test separated from them. Reading Comprehension Test emerged on Evaluation of Semantic Implications (EMI) (*op. cit.* pp.96-97).

The targeted solution of the data of the last study in this series, i.e., the study of Reasoning, Creativity and Evaluation identified more clearly and definitely all the SOI abilities for which there were indications in the original analysis. Two factors: Cognition of Symbolic Classes (CSC) and Evaluation of Semantic Classes (EMC) which did not emerge in the original analysis, emerged in the targeted solution. In the Education of Correlates area, a noteworthy clarification of factors occurred. The tests belonging to Convergent Production of Figural Relations (NFR), Convergent Production of Symbolic Relations (NSR) and Convergent Production of Semantic Relations (NMR), got separated (*op. cit.*, pp.102-103).

The major outcome of these targeted solutions had been to consider 'reasoning in terms of the categories of products, contents and operations of the Guilford's Structure-Of-Intellect (SOI) model as is discussed in the following section.

Induction and Deduction Way Beyond

At the close of Aptitude Research Project (ARP), Guilford considered Thurstone's PMA factors because of their historical importance, in terms of his Structure-Of-Intellect model. He observed that Number Series Test, Letter Series Test, Marks Test, Number Patterns Test, Tabular Combination Test, Secret Writing Test and Letter Grouping Test which marked Cognition of Symbolic Systems (CSS) factor in ARP Studies, were found loaded on Thurstone's Induction factor (I) also. He, therefore, perceived induction as the SOI ability Cognition of Symbolic Systems (CSS). However, Guilford (1972) considered it much too broader than Cognition of Symbolic Systems (CSS) as he stated:

> If Induction is regarded as abstracting or extracting general information from particulars, the term can be defended as applying to all the six products of information. Units have attributes by which they are identified, and those attributes become known through repeated encounters with objects that possess them. Classes, relations, systems and transformations are transposable entities. As such, they are derived through encounters with different individual cases that embody them. Implications come through replicated encounters to which the law of frequency in learning applies. By such reasoning, the concept of induction can be replaced with the operation category of cognition, with many advantages.
>
> (*op. cit.* pp.137-138)

Similarly, for deduction Guilford stated:

> In order to justify the level of deduction a test should take in the completion form, i.e., requiring the subject to produce his own conclusions. As a process deduction should be assigned logically to convergent production, not to evaluation. All the convergent production abilities should be accepted as deductive, in which case that operation could replace completely "deduction" as a process.
>
> (*Ibid.*)

Regarding general reasoning Guilford remarked:

> Thurstone reported a factor which he never recognized as general reasoning, but characterized it as the ability to solve problems when there was a restriction in solution. The same factor later on was called General Reasoning. In SOI model it was identified Cognition of Semantic Systems.
>
> (*Ibid.*)

Thus, Guilford went much beyond in conceptualizing inductive and deductive processes which are involved in any reasoning activity. He identified 'induction' with the – mental operation of cognition and 'deduction' with the mental operation of convergent production. Conceiving these two mental 'operations' interaction upon four kinds of 'contents' – figural, symbolic, semantic and behavioural, each giving six types of 'products' – units, classes, relations, systems, transformations and implications, led to posit forty-eight categories of reasoning ability.

Studies on Reasoning in India

Whatever little research done in India in education or psychology till 1968, was dominated by a concern for the development of various types of psychological and educational tests, mostly tests of general intelligence and achievement, with little concern for the development of test of specific aptitudes like that of 'reasoning' and no concern to attempt basic research to find out their nature. The General Editor of the *Third Indian Year Book of Education on Educational Research* while observing the state of educational research in India till its publication stated this in this way:

> About one-fourth of the studies and investigations in education have been done on measurement and evaluation. These are mainly concerned with the development of various types of psychological and educational tests (most tests of intelligence and achievement), relationship between scores in different subjects, reliability of public examinations and related problems. . . . Basic research in this area has been scarcely attempted so far.
>
> (Adavel, 1968, p.xxii)

The situation did not improve even after 1968 till 1972 when Mitra and Kumar submitted a trend report on the state of research on tests and measurement in the Survey of Research in Education first published in 1974, as they stated:

> A total of only sixty-three studies have so far been awarded Ph.Ds., in test construction and another nineteen have been completed by institution engaged in educational research or psychological research in the country. Maximum number of tests have been devised to assess general intelligence.
>
> (Mitra & Kumar, 1974, p.212)

Anyhow, the first attempt to understand the domain of reasoning in India was made by Sharma (1960) while analyzing a test of reasoning ability consisting of five sub-tests – Grouping, Analogies, Given Facts, Conclusion and Decoding, each with twenty items of multiple choices variety. He administered his tests upon 570 subjects from seven colleges in different parts of India. After analyzing the correlation matrix by centroid method and then by Zimmerman's graphical method of rotation of axes, Sharma identified four factors: General Reasoning, Perception of Relationships, Deduction and Induction. All the five sub-tests had significant loadings on General Reasoning factor. Grouping and Given Facts had substantial loadings on Perception of Relationship factor – a factor Similar to the one identified by Adkins and Lyerly (1952) as 'Perception of Abstract Similarities', and by Green, *et al.*, (1953) as 'Education of Conceptual Relations'. Analogies and Given Facts had loadings on Deduction factor – similar to the factor identified by Thurstone, 1938; Blakey, 1941; and Adkins and Lyerly, 1952. Conclusion had loading on Induction factor – similar to the one, found by Thurstone (1938) and Blakey (1941).

Bala (1977) in a factor analytic study of reasoning ability which she defined in terms of SOI categories of CMC, CMR, CMI, NMC, NMR and NMI, administered nineteen tests representing each of these categories (three for each category, except four for NMI) to 182 thirteen year old, 205 fourteen year old and 153 fifteen year old students in five Government Boys Secondary Schools catering to the children of professional groups – largely Government officials belonging to middle income group in South zone of Delhi. She worked out the principal factor solutions for the correlation matrices for each of the age groups and rotated the axes according to Kaiser's varimax criterion, Cliff's targeted rotation procedure, and finally to oblique rotation fulfilling the quartimin criterion as the earlier rotations could not reveal meaningful and interpretable factors. The first factor which she identified Factor-A: Inference or General Cognition and Convergent Production, through emerged in all the three age groups but its composition varied. The tests belonging to CMI category which had high loadings on Factor-A at the age group 13+, later on emerged on a separate factor identified as Factor-D: Conceptual Foresight or Cognition of Semantic Implications at the age groups 14+ and 15+. Further, tests belonging to NMC category did not have substantial loadings on Factor-A at the age Group 15+. It pointed to the fact that the general factor tended to become less important with increase in age or when the specialized differentiated abilities emerge. Factor-B: Perception of Abstract Similarities or Convergent Production of Semantic Classes and Relations, and Factor-C: Induction or Eduction of Conceptual Relations or Cognition of Semantic Classes and Relations were available at the age group 13+ but their parallels could not be traced at the age groups 14+ and 15+. Perhaps, they shared their variance with Factor-A at the age group 14+, and confounded to form a composite mixed Factor-F: Apprehension of Relations or Mixed Classes and Relations at the age group 15+. This provided evidence for integration of abilities. Factor-D_1: Association or Relational Thinking or Diffused Convergent Production and Cognition of Semantic Implications at the age group 13+, differentiated into Factor-D: Conceptual Foresight or Cognition of Semantic Implication and Factor-E: Deduction or General Convergent Production in the later age groups 14+ and 15+. Thus, Bala (1977) identified one mixed general factor at all the three age levels, two mixed classes and relations factors at the age of 13+, one mixed classes and relations factor at the age of 15+, one mixed convergent production factor at the age of 14+ and 15+, one mixed cognition and convergent production implications factor at the age of 13+, and one SOI factor, CMI at the age of 14+ and 15+.

Chhikara (1982) in an attempt to find out the reasoning abilities related to achievement of concepts in life-sciences, administered a battery of nineteen reasoning tests devised by Bala (1977) and one Concepts Achievement Test in life sciences devised by him, to a representative sample of 200 boys of the age group of 15+ studying in class X in Hindi medium Government Senior Secondary Schools located in urban areas of South Delhi. On factor analysis of the correlation matrix for the nineteen reasoning tests by principal factor analysis method and rotating according to varimax criterion, he identified five orthogonal factors, namely, Factor-A: General Cognition and Convergent Production, Factor-B: Eduction of Relations and Implications, Factor-C: Deduction of Inference or Convergent Production of Semantic Implications, Factor-D: Eduction of Categories and Consequences and Factor E: Deduction of Verbal Concepts or Convergent Production of Semantic Classes. Thus, Chhikara identified one mixed general factor, one mixed relations and implications factor, one mixed classes and implications factor, and two SOI factors, NMC and NMI.

Tewari (1985) in an attempt to investigate the inter-relationship between measures of selected Guilford's SOI of factors and Set Concept Achievement of secondary level students, administered Reasoning Ability Test battery consisting of nineteen tests devised by Bala (1977) and Set Concept Achievement test devised by him, to a representative sample of 205 students of class IX in Hindi Medium Government Boys Senior Secondary Schools located in urban area of South Delhi. The schools were situated amidst colonies where mostly Government servants reside. On factor analysis of the Pearson's product moment correlation coefficients between nineteen reasoning tests by principal factor analysis method and rotating the axes according to varimax criterion, five orthogonal factors emerged. These were: Deductive Reasoning or Convergent Production (Factor-A), Cognition of Semantic Implications (Factor-B), Inductive Reasoning or Cognition (Factor-C), Eduction of Classes and Relations (Factor-D), and Convergent Production of Semantic Implications (Factor-E). Thus, Tewari identified one mixed convergent production factor, one mixed cognition factor, one mixed classes and relations factor, and two SOI factors, CMI and NMI.

Singh (1987) conducted an investigation to find out the relationship of certain concepts in Physical Chemistry with cognition and convergent production of semantic classes, relations, and implications of the morphological model of Structure-Of-Intellect. He administered nineteen reasoning tests devised by Bala (1977) for the SOI factors: CMC, CMR, CMI, NMC, NMR and NMI, and a battery of ten concept achievement tests in physical chemistry devised by him, to 207 class XI students studying Chemistry in the Government Boys Senior Secondary School situated amidst officials' colonies in South District of Delhi. On factor analysis of the Pearson's product moment correlation coefficients between nineteen reasoning tests by principal factor analysis method and rotating the axes according to varimax criterion, he identified six orthogonal factors, viz., Factor-A: Eduction of Categories and Relations, Factor-B: Cognition of Semantic Implications, Factor-C: Deduction of Relations and Implications, Factor-D: Deduction of Categories and Implications, Factor-E: Deduction of Categories and Relations, and Factor-F: Eduction of Categories and Implications. Thus, Singh revealed two mixed classes and relations factors (Factor-A and Factor-E), two mixed classes and implications factors (Factor-D and Factor-F), one mixed relations and implication factor (Factor-C), and one SOI factor, CMI. The study did not reveal any general cognition or convergent production factor, or mixed operations factor.

Tyagi (1987) in an attempt to identify some of the SOI abilities related with achievement in Physics, administered nine reasoning tests devised by Bala (1977) as measures of SOI factors: CMR, NMR and NMI, eight reasoning tests devised by Tyagi himself as measures of SOI factors: CMS, NMS and CMT (three each for CMS and NMS while two for CMT) and an achievement test, namely, *Gati Sankalpna Samprapati Parikshan Patra* also devised by Tyagi himself, to a representative sample of 280 class IX students in Government Boys' Senior Secondary Schools situated in officials' colonies of the middle class people of South Delhi. On factor analysis of Pearson's product moment correlation coefficients between seventeen reasoning tests by principal factor analysis method and rotating the axes according to varimax criterion, he identified four reasoning factors, namely, Factor-A: Deduction of Semantic Relations, Factor-B: Eduction of Conceptual Modulations, Factor-C: Inferring Semantic Systems and Factor-D: Eduction of Semantic Relations. Thus, starting with six SOI factors posited by Guilford as reasoning abilities, Tyagi identified two SOI factors, CMR and NMR, one mixed relations and transformations factor, and one mixed operation systems factor.

Thus, Bala (1977) identified one SOI factor, CMI; Chhikara (1982) identified two SOS factors, NMI and NMC; Tewari (1985) identified two SOS factors, CMI and NMI; Singh (1987) identified one SOI factor, CMI; and Tyagi (1987) identified two SOI factors, CMR and NMR. Other factor identified in these studies were either mixed product factors, and/or mixed operation factors and/or mixed general factors.

An Overview

Looking back apart from *a priori* postulations, the first study conducted in the domain of reasoning in America by Thurstone (1938), identified three reasoning factors: Induction (I), Deduction (D) and Restricted Reasoning (R). After Thurstone abilities, like, Induction, Deduction and Restricted Reasoning were investigated which led some investigators to posit other abilities under reasoning (Guilford & Lacey, 1947; Rimoldi, 1951; Adkins & Lyerly, 1952). The work of Green, *et al.*, (1953); Guilford, *et al.*, (1954); Kettner, *et al.*, (1956); and Kettner, *et al.*, (1959) led Guilford (1972) to posit reasoning in terms of two mental operations – cognition and convergent production, four types of contents of information – figural, symbotic, semantic and behavioural, and six forms of products of information – units, classes, relations, systems transformations and implications, that is, forty-eight categories of reasoning abilities. Instead of rather narrowly conceived two broad mental processes of induction and deduction, this has been perhaps a more meaningful and broader description of the concept of reasoning in terms of empirically defined tasks/abilities.

The study conducted earlier in India or elsewhere did not fully encompass the products of semantic information of both these mental operations in one particular study. Of the five studies conducted in India in this area four, viz., Bala (1977), Chhikara (1982), Tewari (1985) and Singh (1987) used six SOI factors – CMR, CMC, CMI, NMR, NMC and NMI while the fifth one which was conducted by Tyagi (1987), included three of the SOI factors, CMR, NMR and NMI, and three other SOI factors – CMS, CMT and NMS. Thus, altogether, nine SOI abilities were investigated in India. Hence, there was a need to investigate all the twelve SOI factors which cover two mental operations – cognition and convergent production of one content category – semantic and all the six product categories in one study.

Further, in the study conducted in India by Bala (1977), one general mixed factor, one mixed operations factor, five mixed product factors and one SOI factor emerged; in the study conducted by Chhikara (1982), one mixed general factor, two mixed product factors and two SOI factors emerged; in the study conducted by Tewari (1985), three mixed product factors and two SOI factors emerged; in the study conducted by Singh (1987), five mixed product factors and one SOI factor emerged; in the study conducted by Tyagi (1987), one mixed operations factor, one mixed products factor and two SOI factors emerged. When viewed against the debate on heterogeneity and homogeneity of samples of British and American studies (*cf.* Ch. I), it appeared that the criteria of sex, age and/or grade level were not sufficient to treat their samples as homogeneous samples. This suggested a need to form two samples – one on the basis of the sex, age and grade and another not only on the basis of sex, age and grade but also on the basis of 'context' and 'maturation'. In other words this suggested a need to form a heterogeneous and a homogeneous sample in terms of context and maturation, and to study the domain of reasoning separately for them.

3

SELECTION AND CONSTRUCTION OF TESTS

AS SOON as the problem was envisaged and the abilities involved in 'reasoning' as suggested by Prof. Guilford in terms of mental operations of cognition and convergent production, content category of semantic and product categories of units, classes, relations, systems, transformations and implications of his SOI model were selected, a need to identify or to construct suitable measures (tests) for each of these factors (abilities) arose. As these abilities were twelve in number, it required at least thirty-six tests, i.e., three tests for each factor for proper identification of an ability in a factor analytic study.

A tentative list of tests which were found suitable as measures of these twelve SOI reasoning factors, keeping in view their loadings on these factors in the various ARP studies (as reported by Guilford & Hoepfner, 1971 pp.74-89), was prepared. This list was mailed to Prof. Guilford with a request to suggest the names of the tests to be included in the present study. On receipt of Prof. Guilford's advice (Appendix E) and after discussion with various experts, the following tests were finally included in the present study:

Sl.No.	Name of the Test	SOI Factor
1.	Verbal Comprehension	CMU
2.	Word Substitution	CMU
3.	Word Meaning	CMU
4.	*Word Classification	CMC
5.	*Logical Classification	CMC
6.	*Sentence Classification	CMC
7.	*Verbal Analogies	CMR
8.	*Word Linkage Test	CMR
9.	*Word Matrix Test-I	CMR
10.	+Necessary Arithmetic Operation	CMS

Contd.

11.	+Ship Destination	CMS
12.	+Necessary Facts	CMS
13.	+Similarities	CMT
14.	Different Meanings	CMT
15.	+Social Institutions	CMT
16.	*Apparatus Test	CMT
17.	*Effect Test	CMI
18.	*Seeing Problems	CMI
19.	*Pertinent Questions	CMI
20.	Word Group Naming	NMU
21.	Naming Meaningful Trend	NMU
22.	Picture Group Naming	NMU
23.	*Word Grouping	NMC
24.	*Group Classification	NMC
25.	*Figure Concept	NMC
26.	*Verbal Relations Naming	NMR
27.	*Inventive Verbal Relations	NMR
28.	*Association-IV	NMR
29.	+Sentence Order	NMS
30.	+Temporal Order	NMS
31.	+Word Matrix-II	NMS
32.	Gestalt Transformation	NMT
33.	Unusual Uses	NMT
34.	Object Synthesis	NMT
35.	*Syllogisms-III	NMI
36.	*Missing links	NMI
37.	*Sequential Association	NMI

Nineteen of these tests, i.e., those which are market by a asterisk(*) sign were developed by Bala (1977) and eight which are marked by a plus (+) sign were developed by Tyagi (1987).

Bala (1977) had developed eighteen of these tests, i.e., three each for the SOI factors, Cognition of Semantic Classes (CMC), Cognition of Semantic Relations (CMR), Cognition of Semantic Implications (CMI), Convergent Production of Semantic Classes (NMC), Convergent Production of Semantic Relations (NMR) and Convergent Production of Semantic Implications (NMI). One additional test for the SOI factor, Cognition of Semantic Implications (CMI) was also developed by Bala (1977). Subsequently, Tyagi (1987) had developed another set of eight tests, i.e., three for the SOI factor, Cognition of Semantic Systems (CMS), two for the SOI factor, Cognition of Semantic Transformation (CMT) and three for SOI factor Convergent Production of Semantic Systems (NMS). All these tests were found to be satisfactory. Therefore, these were selected to constitute the reasoning ability test-battery for the present investigation. But the remaining ten tests, i.e., three for the SOI factor, Cognition of Semantic Units (CMU), one for the SOI factor, Cognition of Semantic Transformations (CMT), three for SOI factor, Convergent Production of Semantic Units (NMU) and three for the SOI factor, Convergent Production of Semantic Transformation (NMT) were not available. These were constructed by the author himself. In the following sections, an attempt is made first to describe the nature of the SOI reasoning factors covered in the present study and tests used as their measures, and then to describe in detail the procedure used for the construction of tests which were not available.

Description of SOI Reasoning Factors and Their Measures*

Cognition of Semantic Units (CMU)

This factor has been defined as the ability 'to comprehend meanings of words or ideas'. It was first identified by Burt (1915). The most dependable and univocal measure of this ability has been a vocabulary test of some kind. Three tests, viz., Verbal Comprehension, Word Substitution and Word Meanings were the suitable measures of this ability. These were constructed by the author himself.

The Verbal Comprehension Test was a five choices vocabulary test constructed on the principle that an examinee would identify the best synonym out of the five alternatives for an underlined word. In each of the twenty-four items of this test, five verbal concept below an underlined verbal concept were given. The examinees were asked to find out one verbal concept out of those five verbal concepts which had almost the same meaning as that of the underlined verbal concept.

The Word Substitution Test was constructed on the principle that the examinees would identify what he thought to be the best substitute out of four alternative words for the underlined word in a given sentence. In each of the twenty two items of this test, four verbal concepts similar in meaning to an underlined verbal concept in a given sentence were given. The examinees were asked to identify a verbal concept out of the four given verbal concepts which could be the best substitute for the underlined verbal concept.

The Word Meaning Test was constructed on the principle that an examinee had acquaintance with the concept for which a word stood.

* Copies of the tests can be had from the author.

In each of the twenty eight items of this test, one verbal concept was given. The examinees were asked to write the meaning of the verbal concept on the dotted line.

Cognition of Semantic Classes (CMC)

This factor has been defined as the ability 'to recognize common properties of words, ideas and objects'. The tests of abilities pertaining to this factor could be of several standard types. However, three tests, viz., Word Classification, Logical Classification and Sentence Classification devised by Bala (1977) were found to be suitable for the present study.

The Word Classification Test was a test of exclusion type of format. In each of the forty items of this test five verbal concepts, four of which were alike due to some common property and one was different due to same property, were given. An examinee was asked to identify one verbal concept which did not belong to the class to which the rest of the four belonged.

The Logical Classification Test was a test of discrimination format. In each of its fifteen items, one verbal statement was given. Below each verbal statement four verbal labels for that statement were given. An examinee was asked to recognize one verbal label amongst them, which would best describe the statement.

The Sentence Classification Test was a test of discrimination format. In each of the thirty items of this test, one verbal statement was given. The examinees were asked to discriminate or classify those verbal statements into one of the three classes, viz., 'facts', 'possibilities' or 'names'.

Cognition of Semantic Relations (CMR)

This factor has been defined as the ability 'to see relations between ideas or meanings of words'. It fits well with Spearman's concept of 'eduction of relations'. Three tests, namely, Verbal Analogies Test Word Linkage Test and Word Matrix Test devised by Bala (1977), which were all of multiple choice format and mostly used as measures of this ability were used in the present study.

The Verbal Analogies Test had in each of its twenty items two pairs of verbal concepts. In the second pair one verbal concept was missing. Both the verbal concepts in each pair were related in the same way.

The Examinees were required to educe the relationship between the verbal concepts of the first pair and then to find out a verbal concept out of the four given verbal concepts, which would complete the second pair of verbal concepts having similar relation.

The Word Linkage Test had in each of its twenty items, two verbal concepts with a blank space between them. A list of three verbal concepts was also given with each item. The examinees were required to select one verbal concept from the given list of three verbal concepts which would be related through differently to the two given verbal concepts.

The Word Matrix-I Test had in each of its twenty items, two rows of verbal concepts. The first row had three verbal concepts in it while second had two verbal concepts and a blank space in between. Below these rows were given a list of four verbal concepts. The examinee were asked to educe the relationship among the three verbal concepts of the first row and then to select one verbal concept out of the given list of four verbal concepts which when placed in the blank space in the second row would conform to the same relationship as among the verbal concepts of the first row.

Cognition of Semantic System (CMS)

Cognition of Semantic System (CMS) has been defined as the ability 'to comprehend semantically relatively complex ideas or systems'. Thurstone (1938) was the first to identify this factor in his PMA analysis. He identified this factor as Restricted Reasoning because Arithmetic Reasoning Test which had highest loading on it, required solving of arithmetic problems under restrictions. In AAF research, the same factor was called General Reasoning. ARP studies demonstrate that understanding the structure of the problem is the crucial aspect for this ability (*cf.* Guilford, 1967, p.27). Necessary Arithmetic Operation, Ship Destination and Necessary Facts were the three tests suggested by Guilford (*Ibid.*, pp.96-97) as measures of this factor. These tests were devised by Tyagi (1987), and secured from him for the present study.

The Necessary Arithmetic Operation Test had in each of its twenty two items an arithmetical problem with a list of four arithmetical operations or set of operations given below them. An examinee was asked to identify which one of the given operations or set of operations could be used to solve the arithmetic problem (without actually solving it).

The Ship Destination Test consisted of twenty nine items which were to be answered keeping in view a diagram as given in the test in which a letter given inside a circle indicated either a port or a ship. The lines in the diagram indicated the routes from one port to another. The examinees were asked to identify the distance from Ship to port under varying conditions in each item. The needed computations were absolutely very simple.

The Necessary Facts Test had in each of its twenty two items an arithmetical problem of which a certain fact was not given. The examinees were asked to state the missing fact in each item. This test also did not imply any computations. It was designed to see how well an examinee understood the problem as a whole.

Cognition of Semantic Transformations (CMT)

Cognition of Semantic Transformations (CMT) has been defined as the ability to see potential changes of various kinds, i.e., in meaning, interpretation, significance, attributes, role, use etc., in the existing or known verbally described meaningful information. This factor for the first time was identified in the Aptitude Research Project (Kettner *et al.*, 1959; Marks, *et al.*, 1959; Wilson, *et al.*, 1954). Similarities Test and Social Institutions Test were the most consistent marker tests of this ability in these studies (Guilford, 1967, p.102). These were secured from Tyagi (1987). Another test, Different Meanings which was found to be suitable for inclusion in the present study was developed by the author himself.

The Similarities Test was somewhat like a test by the same name in the Wechsler Verbal Scale. It presented a pair of two common objects in each of its ten items and asked the examinees to state three ways in which the pair of common objects were alike.

The Different Meanings Test had eight items, in each of which one verbal concept was given. An examinee was asked to write as many as four verbal concepts which, though similar in meaning to the given verbal concept, are used in different situations.

The Social Institution Test had in each of its twelve items the name of a social institution or a custom. The examinees were asked to suggest two improvements for each of those social institutions or customs. This test was constructed on the principle that in suggesting two improvements in an institution an examinee would modify or enlarge his conception of the given institution as he would have to deal with its different aspects.

Cognition of Semantic Implications (CMI)

Cognition of Semantic Implications has been defined as the ability 'to anticipate, predict, expect or be sensitive to the needs of or the consequences of a given situation in meaningful terms'. It is an ability which comes closer to seeing the cause and effect type of relation. This factor was first identified in connection with a study of planning abilities (Berger, *et al.*, 1957). Four tests, namely, Apparatus Test, Effect Test, Seeing Problems Test and Pertinent Questions Test which were developed by Bala (1977) as measures of this ability, were also found suitable for the present study.

The Apparatus Test had in each of its ten items the name of a common appliance. The examinees were asked to identify two possible improvements in each of the appliances, concerning with their use, working and formation.

The Effect Test had in each of its seven items a statement concerning present day facts or happenings of an event. The examinees were asked to predict/forecast three of the possible future effects.

The Seeing Problem Test had in each of its seven items the name of an object of common use. An examinee was asked to cognize as many as three difficulties/problems that could arise while using the object given in each item. Those difficulties might be concerned with the use, formation, working or other characteristics of the objects but not with getting rid off them.

The Pertinent Question Test was the key test for the SOI factor Cognition of Semantic Implications in a study of planning abilities by Berger, *et al.*, (1957). In each of the eight items of this test, a problem situation involving two options was given. The examinees were asked to state as many as three questions which could help in deciding the course of action in those problem situations.

Convergent Production of Semantic Units (NMU)

Convergent Production of Semantic Units has been defined as the ability 'to converge on an appropriate name or summarizing word for the given semantic information'. It is the most common task in any class room situation when one converging answer to a question is asked either in oral or in written tests (Meeker, 1969, p.81). Three tests, namely, Word Group Naming, Naming Meaningful Trend and Picture Group Naming which were found to be the strongest measure of NMU (Guilford, 1967, p.172-173) were selected for the present investigation. As none of these tests were available, these were constructed by the author himself.

The Word Group Naming Test had in each of its twenty-nine items the names of five objects. The examinees were asked to put them together into an acceptable set (unit) and give it a name or verbal label of which the given five objects could be the proper instances.

The Naming Meaningful Trend Test had in each of its items five or six verbal labels of such animate or inanimate or abstract fundaments which could be arranged in an acceptable trend. The examinees were asked to deduce and name the trend in which these objects were arranged.

The Picture Group Naming Test had in each of its twenty items the line drawings of five animate or inanimate objects. These objects through apparently different had a 'similarity' by virtue of their occurrence, function or use on the basis of which they could be put in a set (unit). The examinees were asked to deduce the set within which they could be put together to give a name to that set.

Convergent Production of Semantic Classes (NMC)

Convergent Production of Semantic Classes has been defined as the ability 'to produce verbally meaningful classes under specific conditions and restrictions' (Meeker, 1969, p.82). This factor for the first time was recognized in a study by Merrifield, *et al.*, (1962). Many Psychologists, like, Bruner, Goodnow and Austin considered the kind of tests involved in tests of NMC to be the basis for 'concept formation' in general (Meeker, 1969, p.82). Educators such as Russell (1956) have stated that in subjects, like Science, Social Studies, English, Foreign Languages, Mathematics and Specific Language Arts, preparation for assimilation depends on this ability. Three tests, namely, Word Grouping, Group Classification and Figure Concept which were found to be suitable for the present study were constructed by Bala (1977).

The Word Grouping Test consisted of a list of ten verbal concepts. The examinees were asked to converge these verbal concepts into four unique classes on the basis of their meaning, such that, no verbal concept appeared in more than one class.

The Group Classification Test consisted two target groups in each of its items. These were followed by a list of eight groups of three words each. The examinees were asked to classify these eight groups of three words each into two classes such that one word of each word-group is related to one word of the other three words groups so classified, and the classes of groups of words so formed were in turn related to any one of the words of the target groups.

The Figure Concepts Test presented line drawings of twenty familiar objects. The examinees were asked to find out qualities or features these objects have in common and to name them. He could form as many classes composed of two objects each, as he could. The same object depending upon its other characteristics could also be used for different grouping.

Convergent Production of Semantic Relations (NMR)

Convergent Production of Semantic Relations (NMR) has been defined as the ability 'to produce a word or idea that conforms to specific relationship requirements'. Thus, it was similar to Spearman's, factor Eduction of Correlates. Three tests, namely, Verbal Relations Naming, Inventive Verbal Relations and Association-IV constructed by Bala (1977), were found to be suitable for inclusion in the present study.

The Verbal Relations Naming Test had in each of its forty items two pairs of verbal concepts each exhibiting same relationship. The examinees were asked to name the relationship in each item.

The Inventive Verbal Relations Test consisted of five parts. In each part, the relationship between the pairs of words of all the four items was specified in the beginning. However, in each item, one word was given while another was missing. The examinees were asked to write the missing word keeping in view the relationship specified in each part.

The Association-IV Test had in each of its twenty items two verbal concepts having a blank space in between them. The examinee were asked to write on the blank space, a verbal concept which was related though differently to both the given verbal concepts.

Convergent Production of Semantic Systems (NMS)

Convergent Production of Semantic Systems (NMS) has been defined as the ability 'to order information into a verbally meaningful sequence'. Three tests, namely, Sentence Order, Temporal Order and Word Matrix-II which were recommended by Guilford (1967, p.177) as measures of this ability and constructed by Tyagi (1987) were used for the present study.

The Sentence Order Test had in each of its twenty items, three or four sentences which stated various episodes of an event but written in a jumbled manner. The examinees were asked to deduce the correct order in which the various episodes could happen.

The Temporal Order Test presented six situations which would require a number of steps in a successive order. Below each situation was given a list of those steps but in scrambled order. The examinees were asked to deduce the appropriate or meaningful serial order of those steps.

The World Matrix-II had in each of its twelve items a matrix of the order of 3×3. Three cells of each of these matrices were already filled in while remaining six were left blank. The examinees were asked to fill them from the list of six words given below each matrix in such a way that the three words common to each row and to each column were connected in a relevant and acceptable way.

Convergent Production of Semantic Transformation (NMT)

Convergent Production of Semantic Transformation (NMT) has been defined as the ability 'to produce new uses for objects by taking them out of their given context and redefining them'. Three tests, namely, Gestalt Transformation, Unusual Uses and Object Synthesis which were found suitable measures of this ability (Guilford, 1967, p.89), were developed by the author himself as these were not available.

The Gestalt Transformation Test had in each of its twenty item, a task which could be accomplished in an unusual way by any one of the four objects given in the alternatives. The examinee were asked to deduce that object which could be used in a novel way to accomplish the given task.

The Unusual Uses Test had in each of its twenty items, the name of an object of daily use and the task for which that object is generally used. The examinees were asked to deduce an unusual task for which the object given in each item could be used.

The Object Synthesis Test had in each of its twenty-four items, the names of two objects. The examinees were asked to deduce and write the name of an object which could be made by combining the two given objects.

Convergent Production of Semantic Implication (NMI)

Convergent Production of Semantic Implications (NMI) has been defined as the ability 'to deduce meaningful information implicit in the given information'. This factor is very close to popular psychological concept of Deduction. A completion type of Syllogistic Test was found to be suitable measure of this factor. The Sequential Association Test was also found to be suitable measure of it (Guilford, 1967, p. 183). Both these tests and an additional test Missing Links constructed by Bala (1977), were used for the present study.

The Syllogisms-III Test had in each of its twenty items, two statements (premises). The examinees were asked to draw a meaningful conclusion on the basis of information given in the two premises in each item.

The Missing Links Test had in each of its ten items two words having three blank spaces in between. The examinees were asked to produce three words and to place them in the blank spaces in such a way that all the five words together formed a chain which started from the first word (given on the left) and ended with the last word (given on the right); each word in this chain was associated with its immediate neighbour in a meaningful way.

The Sequential Association Test had in each of its ten items a list of four words. The examinees were asked to indicate the best order of those four words to produce a chain of association.

Thus, of the thirty-seven tests used for the present study, nineteen were developed by Bala (1977), eight by Tyagi (1987) and ten were developed by the author himself. The procedure for the construction of these ten test is described in the succeeding sections.

Construction of Tests

As stated earlier, three tests, Verbal Comprehension, Word Substitution and Word Meanings as measures of SOI ability Cognition of Semantic Units (CMU) were developed by the author. One test, Different Meanings as measures of SOI ability Cognition of Semantic Transformation (CMT) was also developed by him. Three tests, Word Group Naming, Naming Meaningful Trend and Picture Group Naming as measures of SOI ability Convergent Production of Semantic Units, and three tests, Gestalt Transformation, unusual uses and object synthesis as measures of SOI ability Cognition of Semantic Transformation were also developed. It was found necessary by the present investigator to develop these tests, because suitable measures were not available. As an exploratory exercise, about double the number of items as required for the final tests were constructed. These were assembled into pre-try-out forms, and were informally used on very small groups of class IX students to find out how well they understood the instructions and what were their responses. These pre-try-out tests were also shown to some of the N.C.E.R.T. colleagues and to research supervisor to get some idea bout the adequacy or inadequacy of the material. This enabled the author to drop many of the items, and to modify or change some of the item-stems or choices, or to modify the directions. Preliminary forms of the tests were thus prepared. The items in these forms were arranged according to the ascending order of their difficulty levels as guessed by the author and his colleagues in the N.C.E.R.T. These preliminary forms were then shown to experts for scrutiny and editorial review. The items were then re-arranged, modified or revised according to their suggestions. The try-out tests were thus prepared after sufficient scrutiny and review.

Try-out Sample

To make the try-out sample representative of the population for which the present investigation was to be conducted, it was decided to select a representative sample of class IX students studying in Government Boys Senior Secondary Schools located in South Delhi. From the available list of Government Boys Senior Secondary Schools in South Delhi, five schools which were considered typical of South Delhi schools, were selected. From these five schools, one section each of class IX students was used for the try-out. A sample of 185 students was convenient for working out the upper and lower twenty-seven per cent groups for item analysis using a dichotomous criterion and an available abac (Harper *et al.*, 1962). However, in all there were 204 students in the selected sections of class IX in those schools, but few of the students in each school were absent either on the first day or on the second day of the try-out. The answer-sheets of such students were not included for item analysis. Even after this 188 students took the tests on both the days. The maximum number was forty-two in Moti Bagh School. So, three sheets were picked up randomly by a child which were put aside. This gave 185 answer sheets for item analysis in each test. The names of the schools selected for the try-out, number of students in class IX of the selected sections, number of students who were present on both the days, number of answer-sheets used for item-analysis and dates of try-out are given in Table 3.1.

TABLE 3.1: Names of the try-out schools, dates of try-out, number of students on the roll and number of sheets used for item-analyses

Sl. No.	Name of School	Dates of Try-out	No. of Students		No. Used for item analysis
			in the section	present both days	
01	Government Boys' Senior Secondary School No. 1 Sarojini Nagar	27 & 28 Sept., 83	41	38	38
02	Government Boys' Senior Secondary School, No. 1 Kidwai Nagar	29 Sept. and 1 Oct., 83	39	35	35
03	Government Boys' Senior Secondary School No. 1, Moti Bagh	3 & 4 Oct., 83	43	42	39
04	Government Boys' Senior Secondary School, Begampur	5 & 6 Oct., 83	42	36	36
05	Government Boys' Senior Secondary School, Sector 6, R.K. Puram	10 Aug., and 27 Sept., 83	39	37	37
		Total	204	188	185

Try-out Administration

The students were tested in their respective schools and they were seated quite apart leaving sufficient space in between to avoid copying. With the help of school administration, proper arrangement for light and ventilation at the place of testing was done. Before one or two days of starting the actual test administration students selected in each try-out school were told about the purpose of holding the tests, and to make them familiar with the procedure of answering the items, they were distributed a practice-sheet used by Bala (1977). To each group of students, tests were administered by the author himself. However, to maintain the discipline, class teachers were also present in the halls where testing was done. As soon as a test and its answer sheet was distributed to the students, they were asked to put down the required identification data information on the answer-sheet in case of test-booklet-answersheet format of the test. Otherwise, in case of on-the-booklet format, they had to furnish the required information on the test booklet itself. After this, they were asked to read the general instruction silently while the test administrator read them aloud. These instructions included the procedure for writing the answers (as given in the examples for the test in question). Only when it was ensured that the instructions, procedure for writing the answers and examples were clear to every student, they were told to proceed with answering a test. As soon as the signal for starting a test was given, the author noted down its starting time. Also, as and when a test was completed by about ninety to ninety-five per cent student, the time was noted down by the author again. After completion of a test by all the students, the answer-sheets and test booklets were collected back. The next test was then distributed and its procedure was explained.

All the try-out tests were administered in the same manner to each group of students in different schools in two sessions with an interval of half an hour in between, in the following order:

First Day: Session I

01. Verbal Comprehension Test
02. Gestalt Transformation Test
03. Picture Group Naming Test

Session II

04. Object Synthesis Test
05. Different Meanings Test

Second Day: Session I

06. Naming Meaningful Trend Test
07. Word Group Naming Test
08. Word Substitution Test

Session II

09 Unusual Uses Test
10. Word Meanings Test

Before each try-out administration, any mark or writing on reusable test booklets was completely erased or such booklets which were badly mutilated were substituted by new one's. The try-out administration was done on the dates as indicated in Table 3.1.

Development of Scoring Keys

The reasoning tests constructed for the presented study were of two types, i.e., multiple choice type and completion type. Verbal Comprehension Test, Word Substitution Test and Gestalt Transformation Test were of multiple choice type while Word Meaning Test, Different Meanings Test, Word Group Naming Test, Naming Meaningful Trend Test, Picture Group Naming Test, Object Synthesis Test and Unusual Uses Test were of completion type. The keys for the multiple choices type of tests were prepared by the author himself and two of his N.C.E.R.T. Colleagues independently. These were then compared and discussed, after which final scoring keys were prepared.

For developing scoring keys in case of completion type of tests, a different procedure as used in ARP studies and by Bala (1977) was adopted. A random sample of twenty-five per cent of the answer scripts of the students was drawn and a list of responses for each test item was prepared. A list of responses as per the guidelines for scoring given in Guilford & Hoepfner (1971) for a completion type of test was also prepared. The responses of the twenty-five per cent of the students were evaluated in terms of the list of responses prepared. The responses which were considered proper by the investigator and the criteria of propriety were noted along with their frequency. These were then shown to experts and research supervisor for a thorough review. After considerable discussion criteria for, and, a list of, acceptable responses was prepared. The try-out tests were then scored according to these criteria and acceptable responses. Moreover, in the process of scoring whenever a new response pattern was noted, it was reviewed and if found acceptable, was included in the list.

Proportion of Correct Responses in the Upper and Lower Group

For the purpose of finding out the item difficulty and discrimination indices, the total group which took the try-out tests, was divided into twenty-seven per cent highest scorers and twenty-seven per cent lowest scorers in each test. The group could be divided into upper and lower fourth (twenty five per cent) or thirds (thirty-three per cent) or even halves (fifty per cent), but twenty-seven per cent was found to be the optimum, because it provided the compromise to make the extreme groups as large and as different as possible (Ebel, 1965 pp.348-349). In this, Ebel agreed with Kelley, who showed, ". . . by taking upper and lower groups of twenty-seven per cent of the total group, one can say with the greatest confidence that those in the upper group are superior in the ability measured by the test to those in the lower group" *(Ibid.)*. For, as pointed out by him, "When extreme groups, each consisting of approximately twenty seven per cent of the total group are used, the ratio of the difference in the averages abilities of the groups to the standard error of their difference, i.e., the degree of uncertainty about the size of the real difference, is maximum" (Kelley, 1939). After dividing the groups into twenty-seven per cent highest scorers and twenty-seven per cent lowest scorers on the basis of total scores, a count of the number of pupils who correctly answered the item, number of pupils who wrongly answered the item and number of pupils who omitted the item, was made for each item in each of the multiple choices type of tests. (Items not responded in between the responded items as well as the item after the last responded item were treated as reached but omitted.) The corrected proportions of right responses in both the higher and lower twenty-seven per cent groups were worked out for each item by using Guilford's formula:

$$pc = \frac{R - \dfrac{W-O}{K-1}}{R+W+O}$$

where

pc = corrected proportion of right responses for an item;
R = number of pupils correctly answered the item;
W = number of pupils wrongly answered the item;
O = number of pupils omitted the item; and
K = number of alternative.

In case of completion type of tests, Word Meaning, Word Group Naming, Naming Meaningful Trend, Picture Group Naming, Unusual Uses and Object Synthesis no correction formula was applied to find out the proportions of right responses in the higher and lower twenty seven per cent groups. These were worked out directly as:

$$p = \frac{\text{Number answering item right}}{\text{Number attempting item}}$$

In case of completion type of test, Different Meanings also no correction formula was applied to find out the proportions of right responses in the upper and lower twenty-seven per cent groups, but a slightly different procedure was adopted to work out these. This test required to find out as many as four verbal concepts for each verbal concept given in an item. Therefore, response counts were made for those who gave one right response, two right responses, three right responses and four right responses. Thus, the proportions of right responses in both the higher and lower twenty-seven per cent groups were worked out separately for one right response, two right responses, three right responses and four right responses.

Difficulty and Discrimination Indices

The item discrimination indices are expressed in the form of relationship between a test-item scores and the total scores on the test (or on an external criterion). Finding out a measure of this relationship, like, product moment correlation coefficient 'r' for each item is a time consuming task. Flanagan (1939) suggested an economical way to find out the values of 'r_s' by using twenty-seven per cent cases at each tail of the distribution. He provided tables for estimating these values for various proportions of correct responses in upper and lower twenty-seven per cent of cases. Davis (1946) translated Flanagan's tables which represented non-linear 'r' into linear scale of discrimination values ranging from 0 to 100 by using Fishers Z. Harper, *et al.* (1962) translated Davis tables into a chart or abac. They plotted Davis linear discrimination values directly on their chart. However, for plotting difficulty values (which are expressed as proportion of passing an item) Harper, *et al., (Ibid.)* instead of using Davis linear discrimination values directly; obtained Fan's (1952) difficulty values and then translated them to linear difficulty values by using Table IV from Davis (1946) book. The discrimination and difficulty values for the different try-out tests, were read from the chart developed by Harper, *et al.*, (1962).

Item Selection

As suggested by Harper, *et al.*, (1962), items which had linear difficulty values between 20 to 80, were considered for inclusion in the final tests in the first instance while the items which had higher proportion of correct responses in the lower twenty-seven per cent group or negative proportion of correct responses in the higher twenty-seven per cent group; or in both the higher and lower twenty seven per cent groups were outrightly rejected. The items having linear difficulty indices between 20 to 80 were evaluated for retaining in the final test in terms of their discrimination powers according to the criteria suggested by Ebel (1965, p.364) which are reproduced in Table 3.2.

TABLE 3.2: Criteria suggested by Ebel for retaining the items in terms of discrimination values (non-linear)

If index is	Do this
0.40 and Up	Accept the item.
0.30 and 0.39	Accept, scrutinize for improvement.
0.20 to 0.29	May be used as marginal, scrutinize for improvement.
0.19 or lower	Reject, revise item.

Scrutinizing the items which had non-linear discrimination values in between 0.20 to 0.29 for improvement required some more time, therefore, only those items which had non-linear discrimination values higher than 0.29 from the items having linear difficulty values between 20 to 80 were retained for inclusion in the final tests. Further, as was stated earlier that the discrimination and difficulty values for the various items in the try-out tests were read from the chart developed by Harper, *et al.*, (1962), it was necessary to find out Harper's linear discrimination value equivalent to non-linear discrimination value of 0.29. Again, it was observed from the linear graph given by Harper, *et al.*, (1962, p.8) that a linear discrimination value of 20 had a value of '*r*' (non-linear discrimination value), somewhere little lower than in the middle of 0.30 and 0.35. So, the criterion for retaining the items was fixed as a linear discrimination value equal to or higher than 20. This criterion was found to be very satisfactory as it rejected all those item which fell in the lower bound of 0.30 and 0.39 because as per Ebel's suggestion they required improvement.

Anstey (1966, p.42), it was decided to set the time limits that around ninety-five per cent of the students could complete a test. The same criterion was used by Bala (1977) and Tyagi (1987). The frequency distributions of the time taken to complete each of the try-out tests were therefore made and ninety-fifth percentiles were computed. The estimate to time for each of the final tests was made by adjusting the time limits according to the number of items finally selected. The estimated time for each test is shown in Table 3.3.

TABLE 3.3: Calculation of time for the final forms of the tests

Sl. No.	Name of Test	No. of Items in Try-out Test	Time Taken by 95% of the pupils (min.)	No. of Items in the final Test	Estimated Time (rounded Off) (min.)
01	Verbal Comprehension	45	29	24	15
02	Gestalt Transformation	42	32	20	15
03	Picture Group Naming	38	29	20	15
04	Object Synthesis	42	34	24	20
05	Different Meanings	11	22	8	15
06	Naming Meaningful Trend	35	22	30	20
07	Word Group Naming	43	30	29	20
08	Word Substitution	40	19	22	10
09	Unusual Uses	42	27	24	15
10	Word Meanings	47	26	28	15

Final Battery of Reasoning Tests

The final battery of reasoning tests for this study consisted of thirty-seven tests. Nineteen of these tests, i.e. those involving Cognition of Semantic Classes (CMC), Cognition of Semantic Relations (CMR), Cognition of Semantic Implications (CMI), Convergent Production of Semantic Classes (NMC), Convergent Production of Semantic Relations (NMR) and Convergent Production of Semantic Implications (NMI) were constructed by Bala (1977). Eight tests involving Cognition of Semantic Systems (CMS), Cognition of Semantic Transformations (CMT) and Convergent Production of Semantic Systems (NMS) were constructed by Tyagi (1987). The remaining tests, i.e., those involving Cognition of Semantic Units (CMU), Cognition of Semantic Transformations (CMT), Convergent Production of Semantic Units (NMU) and Convergent Production of Semantic Transformations (NMT) were constructed by the author. Thus, all these tests together encompassed the full range of reasoning abilities suggested by Guilford for the semantic information.

Arrangement of Tests in the Battery

Various alternatives to arrange the tests in the battery were worked out. But as the total test battery required a minimum of fourteen hours of testing time (includes the time for test administration, reading out the instructions, distribution and collection of test material etc.). The only viable arrangement to utilize the time properly, seemed to be, to arrange cognition tests first and then convergent production tests and then to arrange units tests first, classes tests second, relations tests third, systems tests fourth, transformations tests fifth and implications tests last. So, the total testing time could be spread over seven test sessions and administration of test could be done as per the arrangement given below in Table 3.4.

TABLE 3.4: Arrangement of tests in the battery

Test Sessions	Sl. No.	SOI Factor	Name of the Test	Test-time (Minutes)	
1	2	3	4	5	
Session-I	01	CMU	Verbal Comprehension	15	
	02	CMU	Word Substitution	10	
	03	CMU	Word Meaning	15	
	04	CMC	Word Classification	10	
	05	CMC	Logical Classification	08	
	06	CMC	Sentence Classification	15	73
Session-II	07	CMR	Verbal Analogies	10	
	08	CMR	Word Linkage	10	
	09	CMR	Word Matrix-I	10	
	10	CMS	Necessary Arithmetic Operations	20	
	11	CMS	Ship Destination	15	
	12	CMS	Necessary Facts	16	81
Session-III	13	CMT	Similarities	15	
	14	CMT	Different Meanings	15	
	15	CMT	Social Institutions	16	
	16	CMI	Apparatus Test	20	
	17	CMI	Effects Test	20	86

Contd.

TABLE 3.4 *Contd.*

1	2	3	4	5	
Session-IV	18	CMI	Seeing Problems	20	
	19	CMI	Pertinent Questions	20	
	20	NMU	Word Group Naming	20	
	21	NMU	Naming Meaningful Trend	20	80
Session-V	22	NMU	Picture Group Naming	15	
	23	NMC	Word Grouping	10	
	24	NMC	Group Classification	10	
	25	NMC	Figure Concepts	10	
	26	NMR	Verbal Relations Naming	15	
	27	NMR	Inventive Verbal Relations	20	80
Session-VI	28	NMR	Association-IV	15	
	29	NMS	Sentence Order	12	
	30	NMS	Temporal Order	20	
	31	NMS	Word Matrix-II	20	
	32	NMT	Gestalt Transformation	15	82
Session-VII	33	NMT	Unusual Uses	15	
	34	NMT	Object Synthesis	20	
	35	NMI	Syllogisms-III	20	
	36	NMI	Missing Links	10	
	37	NMI	Sequential Association	10	75

4

FORMATION OF SAMPLES AND COLLECTION OF DATA

THE UNION Territory of Delhi is divided into five zones, viz., south, north, east, west and central. Out of these, south zone consists of the largest number of inhabitants who work in various government, semi-government or similar such departments or institutions. If, as perceived by Prof. V.K.R.V. Rao, Delhi is an inflated official colony, then south zone can well be presumed to provide typical samples of Delhi's population. Both heterogeneous and homogeneous samples for the study were, therefore, confined to the south zone of Delhi.

The Heterogeneous Sample

All the Government Boys' Senior Secondary Schools located in South Delhi have similar infrastructural facilities and their teachers are transferable from one school to another. A few of these schools located in various colonies provide typical sample of student population of those and nearby colonies. After a discussion with E.V.G. Counsellors attached with the various Government Boys' Senior Secondary Schools of South Delhi, educational authorities and researchers, who have familiarity with these schools, the consensus was that Government Boys' Senior Secondary Schools of Begampur, Srinivaspuri, Andrews Ganj, Sarojini Nagar No. 1, Kidwai Nagar No. 1, R.K. Puram, Sector-3 (Morning), R.K. Puram, Sector-3 (Evening), R.K. Puram, Sector-2, R.K. Puram, Sector-6, and R.K. Puram, Sector-7 would provide a typical sample of student population of Delhi. The number of schools from the residential colony of R.K. Puram being more because, it being the largest residential colony, represented a major segment of student population of Delhi. The maximum number of fourteen year old students in these schools were studying in class IX, which had four to five sections in each school. It was therefore decided to select one section of class IX students from each of these schools. Moreover from the selected section, those boys who were not fourteen year old on the first of test administration were not included in the sample. Thus, the heterogeneous sample for the present investigation consisted of fourteen year old class IX students of Government Boys' Senior Secondary School, Begampur, Srinivaspuri, Andrews Ganj, Sarojini Nagar No. 1, Kidwai Nagar No. 1, R.K. Puram, Sector-2, R.K. Puram, Sector-3 (Morning) R.K. Puram, Sector-3 (Evening) R.K. Puram, Sector-6, and R.K. Puram, Sector-7.

The Homogeneous Sample

In order to preclude the possibility of effects due to such moderator variables as social class, income, professional status and the likes on individual differences in reasoning abilities, it was decided to draw the pupils for the homogeneous sample from only one official colony of South Delhi, i.e., R.K. Puram. People living in the residential colony of R.K. Puram were mostly in middle level of government jobs and had almost same type of housing pattern and equivalent community interaction facilities. Thus pupils from the five Government Boys' Senior Secondary Schools of R.K. Puram, selected earlier for the heterogeneous sample, were considered to be good as a homogeneous sample. However, a more objective procedure in terms of between and within schools variation on a criterion more relevant for reasoning abilities, was worked out for the formation of the homogeneous group of pupils.

The scores on Raven's Standard Progressive Matrices (SPM) for the pupils in the heterogeneous sample were collected from the E.V.G. Counsellors attached to these schools. These scores were considered to be appropriate for forming the homogeneous group as Spearman (1938) and Vernon (1942, 1947) both described Raven's SPM scores to be the purest and best measures of '*g*' or general intellectual functioning (Raven, *et al.*, 1983, p.11). Further, Rimoldi (1948); Boyd and Ward (1966) after factor analyzing SPM scores observed that most of their variance was accounted for by a factor called 'induction' which was described to be the major factor under the domain of reasoning (*cf.* Ch. II). Thus, they could well be presumed to be directly related with reasoning abilities. Therefore, to pick out a homogeneous group of schools SPM scores were used. The means and standard deviations of the SPM scores for each school were worked out. These are given in Table 4.1.

TABLE 4.1: Schoolwise Means and Standard Deviations (SDs) of SPM scores

Sl.No.	Name of the School	Sample size	Mean	S.D.
1.	Government Boys' Senior Sec. School, R.K. Puram, Sector-2	49	31.67	5.14
2.	Government Boys' Senior Sec. School, R.K. Puram, Sector-3 (Morning)	48	31.27	4.87
3.	Government Boys' Senior Sec. School, R.K. Puram, Sector-3 (Evening)	18	29.28	4.70
4.	Government Boys' Senior Sec. School, R.K. Puram, Sector-6	29	32.97	4.90
5.	Government Boys' Senior Sec. School, R.K. Puram, Sector-7	20	30.40	6.42
6.	Government Boys' Senior Sec. School, Begampur	41	36.70	8.92
7.	Government Boys' Senior Sec. School, Srinivaspuri	32	28.31	5.92
8.	Government Boys' Senior Sec. School, Andrews Ganj	22	28.27	4.79
9.	Government Boys' Senior Sec. School, Sarojini Nagar No. 1	36	40.81	6.14
10.	Government Boys' Senior Sec. School, Kidwai Nagar No. 1	30	32.33	6.62

As the study required identification of the schools which may be as homogeneous as possible in terms of SPM scores, critical ratios for the significance of difference between different pairs of schools means were worked out by applying Student's '*t*' test. These are given in Table 4.2.

It may be observed from Table 4.2 that Government Boys' Senior Secondary Schools of R.K. Puram, Sector-2, Sector-3 (Morning), Sector-6 and Sector-7, and Kidwai Nagar No. 1 formed a cluster of homogeneous schools, as '*t*' ratios of the significance of difference between mean scores for these schools were found to be not significant at 5 per cent level.

The differences between the variations within schools also lead to formation of a non-homogeneous group. Therefore, Fisher '*F*' test for the equality of two variances was also applied to find out the schools homogeneous in terms of within variations. The critical ratios between different pairs of variances within schools obtained on applying Fisher's '*F*' test are given in Table 4.3.

TABLE 4.2: Student's 't' Ratios Between Different Pairs of School Means

Sl. No.	Name of the School	(1)	(2)	(3)	(4)	(5)	(6)	(7)	(8)	(9)	(10)
1.	Government Boys' Senior Sec. School, R.K. Puram, Sector-2	—	0.39	1.35	1.11	0.49	3.20*	2.63*	2.68*	7.25*	0.40
2.	Government Boys' Senior Sec. School, R.K. Puram, Sector-3 (Morning)		—	1.49	1.49	0.53	3.48*	2.35*	2.38*	7.69*	0.69
3.	Government Boys' Senior Sec. School, R.K. Puram, Sector-3 (Evening)			—	2.53*	0.60	4.12*	0.63	0.65	7.54*	1.77
4.	Government Boys' Senior Sec. School, R.K. Puram, Sector-6				—	1.48	2.25*	3.35*	3.40*	5.72*	0.49
5.	Government Boys' Senior Sec. School, R.K. Puram, Sector-7					—	3.10*	1.15	1.18	7.61*	0.96
6.	Government Boys' Senior Sec. School, Begampur						—	2.76*	4.84*	12.38*	1.32
7.	Government Boys' Senior Sec. School, Srinivaspuri							—	0.03	8.50*	2.45*
8.	Government Boys' Senior Sec. School, Andrews Ganj								—	8.59*	2.48*
9.	Government Boys' Senior Sec. School, Sarojini Nagar No. 1									—	5.43*
10.	Government Boys' Senior Sec. School, Kidwai Nagar No. 1										—

* Significant at 5 per cent level of significance.

TABLE 4.3: Fisher's 'F' Ratios for the Equality of Two Variances

Sl. No.	Name of the School	(1)	(2)	(3)	(4)	(5)	(6)	(7)	(8)	(9)	(10)
1.	Government Boys' Senior Sec. School, R.K. Puram, Sector-2	—	1.11	1.20	1.10	1.56	3.01*	1.33	1.15	1.43	1.66
2.	Government Boys' Senior Sec. School, R.K. Puram, Sector-3 (Morning)		—	1.07	1.01	1.74	3.35*	0.68	1.03	1.59	1.85
3.	Government Boys' Senior Sec. School, R.K. Puram, Sector-3 (Evening)			—	1.09	1.87	3.60*	1.59	1.04	1.71	1.98
4.	Government Boys' Senior Sec. School, R.K. Puram, Sector-6				—	1.72	3.31*	1.46	1.05	1.57	1.83
5.	Government Boys' Senior Sec. School, R.K. Puram, Sector-7					—	1.93	1.18	1.80	1.10	1.06
6.	Government Boys' Senior Sec. School, Begampur						—	2.27*	3.47*	2.11*	1.82
7.	Government Boys' Senior Sec. School, Srinivaspuri							—	1.53	1.08	1.25
8.	Government Boys' Senior Sec. School, Andrews Gunj								—	1.64	1.01
9.	Government Boys' Senior Sec. School, Sarojini Nagar No. 1									—	1.16
10.	Government Boys' Senior Sec. School, Kidwai Nagar No. 1										—

* Significant at 5 per cent level of significance.

It may be observed from Table 4.3 that the '*F*' ratios for the different pairs of Government Boys' Senior Secondary Schools of R.K. Puram, Sector-2, Sector-3 (Morning), Sector-6 and Sector-7, and Kidwai Nagar No. 1 were also not significant at 5 per cent level. This indicated that a homogeneous group can be formed out of the Government Boys' Senior Secondary Schools of R.K. Puram, Sector-2, Sector-3 (Morning), Sector-6, and Sector-7 and Kidwai Nagar No. 1. Such a sample would be a homogeneous sample of fourteen years old class IX students in terms of within school variations in general intellectual functioning. However, keeping in view that the residential colony of R.K. Puram being the largest colony of Government employees belonging to similar kind of subordinate services of the central Government having almost equivalent level of educational, economic and living standards, the socio-cultural background of these people could also be presumed equivalent. Therefore, in order to preclude the possible effects of moderator variables, pupils studying in Government Boys' Senior Secondary School No. 1, Kidwai Nagar, were excluded from the homogeneous sample. Thus, fourteen years old class IX pupils studying in Government Boys' Senior Secondary Schools of R.K. Puram, Sector-2, Sector-3 (Morning), Sector-6 and Sector-7 constituted the homogeneous sample for the study.

Administration of the Tests

Keeping in view the purpose of the investigation, data were collected by administering thirty-seven tests discussed earlier, in each selected school separately to secure measures of various reasoning abilities. Before administration of tests, Deputy Director of Education (South Zone), Delhi Administration was contacted to accord permission. As soon as the permission was accorded, a meeting was held with the school Principals to decide about the dates and timings of the test administration. The School Principals were also requested to provide one teacher during test sessions for proper management and discipline. In each school the tests were administered by the author himself. As the number of students to whom the tests were administered ranged from eighteen to forty-nine, the author did not face any difficulty in maintaining proper test atmosphere. Moreover, the presence of a school teacher during test sessions made the task of maintaining the proper test atmosphere easy. In order to build rapport with the examinees and to orient them for proper test-behaviour, they were explained the purpose and procedure of the test administration. A separate practice sheet together with an answer-sheet was distributed to the examinees before test administration. They were told how to fill up the identification data, and then the way to respond to the test-booklet-answer-sheet format and on-the-booklet format of the tests. Each test whether of structured, semi-structured or of supply-the-answer type had specific directions and examples which were read aloud, and if necessary, were discussed with them. During actual test administration, the subjects were asked to fill up identification data on the answer-sheet first and then the test-booklets for that test were distributed. In case of respond-on-the-test-booklet format, the examinees were also asked to write the identification data first. After this, instructions and examples were read aloud the explained to them. A test was started only when the procedure for attempting its items was clear to each and every examinee. The time limits for each test were strictly observed. The plan of administration of thirty-seven tests required around fourteen hours of testing time, including the time for instructions, examples, distribution and collection of test booklets and answer-sheets. This was spread over seven days and test administration in each school was done for seven days according to the order and arrangement as discussed earlier (Table 3.4, Ch. 3). The schedule of test administration in each school is given in Table 4.4.

Scoring of the Answer-sheets

As anticipated, a small number of students in each school for one reason or another, were unable to complete all the tests. By the omission of such students, the answer-sheets of only those students, who completed all the thirty-seven tests, were retained for scoring. The number of students, who completed all the tests, was 325 in the heterogeneous sample and 146 in the homogeneous sample. The multiple choices type of tests were scored on the computer installed at the N.C.E.R.T. Campus. The total score obtained by a student on a multiple choice type of test was worked out by the following formula:

$$\text{Total Score} = R - \frac{W}{K-1}$$

where, R = Number of right choices;
W = number of wrong choices;
K = number of choices for each item in the test.

TABLE 4.4: Schedule of Test Administration

Sl. No.	Name of School	Dates of Test Administration
1.	Government Boys' Senior Sec. School, R.K. Puram, Sector-3 (Morning)	Nov. 15, 16, 17, 20, 21, 26 & 28, 1984
2.	Government Boys' Senior Sec. School, R.K. Puram, Sector-3 (Evening)	Nov. 15, 16, 17, 20, 21, 26 & 28, 1984
3.	Government Boys' Senior Sec. School, R.K. Puram, Sector-2	Nov. 29, Dec. 3, 4, 5, 6, 7 & 8, 1984
4.	Government Boys' Senior Sec. School, R.K. Puram, Sector-6	Nov. 29, Dec. 3, 4, 5, 6, 7 & 8, 1984
5.	Government Boys' Senior Sec. School, Begampur	Jan. 7, 8, 9, 10, 11, 14 & 15, 1985
6.	Government Boys' Senior Sec. School, R.K. Puram, Sector-7	Jan. 15, 16, 17, 18, 19, 21 & 22, 1985
7.	Government Boys' Senior Sec. School, Srinivaspuri	Jan. 23, 24, 28, 29, 30, Feb. 1 & 2, 1985
8.	Government Boys' Senior Sec. School, Andrews Gang	Jan. 23, 24, 28, 29, 30, Feb. 1 & 2, 1985
9.	Government Boys' Senior Sec. School, Sarojini Nagar No. 1	Feb. 5, 6, 7, 8, 9, 11 & 12, 1985
10.	Government Boys' Senior Sec. School, Kidwai Nagar No. 1	Feb. 5, 6, 7, 8, 9, 11 & 12, 1985

In case of semi-structured supply-the-answer type of tests, scoring of the answer-sheets was done by the author himself according to the specifications of acceptable responses worked out by Bala (1977) and Tyagi (1987) and by the author. The total score obtained by a student on such a test was equal to total count of his acceptable responses.

Tabulation of Data

Each subject in the heterogeneous sample, as well as in the homogeneous sample, was given a serial number separately. These serial numbers were written in the first column of the sheets of paper. In the second and subsequent columns, the test scores of the pupils were written according to the order of administration of tests described earlier (Table 3.4, Ch. 3). Each row of these sheets indicated the score obtained by a pupil in each of the thirty-seven tests. The data from these sheets was punched on IBM cards by the Data Processing Unit of the N.C.E.R.T. These punched cards along with their punching design were given to the Computer Centre, Council for Social Development,

Lodi Estate, New Delhi, for finding out the correlation coefficients, principal factors and varimax rotated factors.

The Reliability Coefficients

The reliability coefficients for each of the thirty-seven tests were worked out by using K-R formula 21 (Guilford, 1954, p. 381). Though a large number of these reliability coefficients as indicated in Appendix A were satisfactory, but a few of them were low. Many psychometricians opine that for useful measurement, a test should achieve a high reliability; while Guilford advocated, " . . . no hard and fast rules could be stated about the size of the reliability coefficients . . . We are frequently faced with the choice of making the best of what reliability we can get, even though, it may be of the order of only 0.50, or going without the use of the test at all. For some purpose, even a test of low reliability adds enough to prediction to justify its use, particularly when used in a battery alongwith other tests. Sometimes even it is quite high, it can give the test user a false sense of security" (Guilford, 1954, p. 388). Guilford, therefore, emphasized that high reliability should not always be regarded as a goal in and of itself for evaluation of tests, especially in multivariate analysis (Guilford, 1946, p.428).

On the other hand, under any assumption, an estimated reliability coefficient vary from one population to another and depend upon other factors, including testing conditions and scoring formula. Therefore, in some cases, the internal-consistency may be low. Guilford was, therefore, of the view, ". . . instead of reliability, factorial validity of a test or its factor-loading should become indispensable facts to know about a test" *(Ibid.)*. Kenny (1958) also shared Guilford's view while pointing out, "Changes in the reliability of the test are not relevant; they may alter the overall size of factor loadings, but should not affect factorial structure".

Moreover, KR-21 formula of estimating the internal consistency reliability provides lower bound estimate and the main aim of the present investigation was to find out the factorial composition of various reasoning tests. So, low reliability coefficients for a few tests were not given much consideration as they would not affect the 'factorial structure'.

Thus, 325 punched cards, one each for the pupils in the heterogeneous sample and 146 punched cards, one each for the pupils in the homogeneous sample, were given separately, to the Computer Centre, Council for Social Development, Lodi Estate, New Delhi, for finding out the correlation coefficients, principal factors and varimax factors, which are discussed in the next chapter.

5

STRUCTURE OF REASONING ABILITY

Correlation Coefficients

THE CORRELATION coefficients are the basics to understand the factorial composition of tests. They serve as basic data for factor-analysis too. The correlation coefficients between all the thirty-seven tests of the study were worked out separately for the heterogeneous and homogeneous samples by using Karl Pearson's product moment correlation coefficient formula (Ferguson, 1966, pp.110-111) as both the assumptions of linearity of regressions of variables and normality of distributions for its use had been well established in the earlier studies (Bala, 1977: Chhikara, 1982; Tewari, 1985; Singh, 1987; Tyagi, 1987). The calculations were done on REYAD/1033 computer. These correlation coefficients are given in Appendix B and Appendix C for the heterogeneous and homogeneous samples respectively.

It was observed from these correlation matrices that almost all the correlations between the tests were fair sized and positive, barring a few which were low sized or not significant. There was no significant correlations which was negative. The reasoning abilities as measured by the present set of tests, therefore, belonged to a positive manifold, both in case of heterogeneous as well as homogeneous sample.

As far as within SOI category-wise inter-correlations are concerned, in case of heterogeneous sample it was observed that thirty-eight out of thirty-nine correlation coefficients among the tests belonging to the same SOI category (except one correlation in case of NMI) were positive and significant at five per cent level of significance; but majority of them were low, and a few fair sized (maximum correlation coefficient being 0.694). Similarly, in case of homogeneous sample, thirty-three out of thirty-nine correlation coefficients among the tests belonging to the same SOI category (except six correlations in case of NMC, NMI and NMT were positive and significant at five per cent level of significance, but majority of them were low, and a few fair-sized (maximum being 0.634). These positive and significant but low to fair sized correlation coefficients among tests of a particular SOI category in case of both the samples indicated that they were not only viable measures of that category but at the same time, the correlations being low to fair sized, they provided measures of different facets of that category.

As far as the correlation coefficients between tests belonging to different Structure-Of-Intellect (SOI) categories were concerned, quite a few of them were not significant. For instance, in case of the heterogeneous sample four correlations of the Logical Classification Test (CMC) with tests belonging to other SOI categories were not significant. Similarly, thirteen correlations of the Apparatus Test (CMI) with tests belonging to other SOI categories were not significant. Again, three correlations of the Gestalt Transformation Test (NMT) with tests belonging to other SOI categories were not significant. Lastly, sixteen correlations of Sequential Association Test (NMI) with tests belonging to other SOI categories were not significant.

On the other hand, in case of homogeneous sample, a large number of these correlations were not significant. For instance, thirteen correlations of Logical Classification Test (CMC) with tests belonging to other SOI categories were not significant. Similarly, eight correlations of Sentence Classification Test (CMC), fifteen correlations of Verbal Analogies Test (CMR), one correlation of Ship Destination Test (CMS), seven correlations of similarities Test (CMT), three correlations of Different Meaning Test (CMT), thirteen correlations of Apparatus Test (CMI), five correlations of Naming Meaningful Trend Test (NMU), nineteen correlations of Group Classification Test (NMC), five correlations of Association-IV Test (NMR), nine correlations of Temporal Order Test (NMS), twelve correlations of Gestalt Transformation Test (NMT), five correlations of Unusual Uses Test (NMT), one correlation of Object Synthesis Test (NMT), six correlations of Missing Links Test (NMI) and finally, thirty-two correlations of Sequential Association Test (NMI) with tests belonging to other SOI categories were not significant.

Thus, out of 666 correlations, thirty-six correlations in case of heterogeneous sample and 159 correlations in case of homogenous sample were not significant. This indicated that various independent dimensions or facets of reasoning abilities were involved and differential identification of these in terms of number increased with the homogeneity of the sample. However, to determine the number of these dimensions and to have a clear understanding of their nature, a more precise procedure of 'factor analysis' of the correlation matrices for both the heterogeneous and homogeneous samples separately had to be adopted. Accordingly, the inter-correlation matrices were subjected to factor analysis.

Factor Analyses

The correlation matrices given in Appendix C and Appendix D for the heterogeneous and homogeneous samples respectively were factor analysed by using principal factor extraction method. The calculations were done on REYAD/1033 computer by using 5.01 version of the programme given for this purpose by Nie, *et al.*, (1975). The computer programme first determined eigen values after assigning ls' in the diagonal entries of the correlation matrices. It then determined communality estimates by taking into consideration the amount of variance contributed to each variable by the principal components whose eigen values were greater than one. The communality estimates were then put in place of ls' to get the reduced correlation matrices (as suggested by Kaiser, 1966). From the reduced correlation matrices principal factors, whose number was equal to the number of eigen values greater than one, were extracted.

Principal factors obtained in this way were only mathematical entities and as such not interpretable. It was therefore, desirable to rotate them in order to make them interpretable and at the same time mathematically equivalent.

Various methods of rotation of factors have been suggested, but 'analytic methods' are mostly preferred as they are based on objectively formulated well defined criteria which ensure reproducibility of the same results. Besides, at no stage in the analytic rotation an investigator can influence the results. Further, these methods can be programmed for a computer (*cf.* Comrey, 1973, p. 168). Several such methods were proposed in the fifties (Carrol, 1963; Ferguson, 1954; Neuhaus and Wrigley, 1954; Saunders, 1960) which appeared to be rather similar to Harman and he referred them collectively as the 'quartimax method' (Harman, 1967, p. 298). These methods attempt to maximize the variance of the squared factor loadings by rows. Thus, they rotate the factors in such a way that ideally each variable gets its major loading in only one factor, i.e., each variable tends to emerge as a pure factor measure. However, most of the time, these methods tended to provide a general factor with which all or most of the variables are substantially correlated. Thus, the idealised solutions proposed by the 'quartimax method' remained only a dream. This led Kaiser (1958) to propose 'varimax method', which is perhaps the most popular rotational procedure in use. It maximizes the variance of the squared factor loadings by columns and leaves some of the variables on a factor with high loadings, a few with intermediatory loadings while quite a lot of them with very low sized loadings. Thus, it offers easy interpretability of a factor, because the factor is similar in nature to the variables with high loadings and not with variables with low loadings. The intermediate sized loadings in such a case do not contribute much for interpretation of the factor (*cf.* Comrey, 1973, p. 173). Thus, varimax method suggested by Kaiser (1958, 1959) was adopted for rotation of the mathematically derived factors in the present investigation. The same computer programme which was used to extract unrotated principal factors, was used to obtain varimax orthogonal rotated factors. The results are discussed separately for the heterogeneous and homogeneous samples in the following sections.

Results for the Heterogeneous Samples

The eigen values in descending order of their magnitudes for the complete correlation matrix in case of heterogeneous sample are given in Table I, Appendix D. It was observed from this table that out of thirty-seven eigen values, only seven were greater than one. This suggested that the number of relevant factors necessary to explain the total communality among the thirty-seven variables, must be upto seven. The communality estimates for each of the thirty-seven variables from the first seven principal components were then worked out; followed by seven principal factors after inserting the communality estimates in the diagonal entries of the correlation matrix given in Appendix B. The seven principal factors so obtained and the estimated communality for each variable are given in Table II, Appendix D. It was observed from the table that Factor-1 had almost all the loadings to be negative while other factors had roughly half of the positive and half of the negative loadings. Besides this, each variable had positive as well as negative loadings. Also, each variable had loadings on more than one factor. This complex over-lapping coupled with bi-polarity made it difficult to explain the nature of factors and to use that description for understanding the pattern of reasoning abilities. Therefore, as discussed earlier in order to make the factors interpretable, these factors were rotated according to varimax criterion. The orthogonal rotated factors obtained by using this criterion and given in Table III, Appendix D.

Tables 5.1 to 5.7 given below describe the nature of each of the seven varimax rotated factors. These tables have been gleaned from Table III, Appendix D. In these tables, a test which had its significant loading on one factor only, is marked by two asterisks(**) in the table of loadings of a factor on which it had its significant loading. All such tests on a factor are relatively pure factor measures and best 'marker tests' which help to identify the nature of that factor. Therefore, they are called defining tests for that factor (Comrey, 1973, pp. 190-91). Further in these tables, a test which had significant loadings on more than one factor, is marked by one asterisk (*) in the table of loadings of a factor on which it had its highest loading. All such tests are complex variables and they are apt to have moderate loadings on several factors. Therefore, they are not helpful in identifying the nature of the factor on which they have marked loadings *(Ibid.)*. The size of the loading of a test on a factor is also very important for interpretation purpose. Comrey (1973, p.226) rated a loading of 0.71 and above as excellent; a loading of 0.63 and above as very good; a loading of 0.55 and above as good; a loading of 0.45 and above as fair; and a loading below 0.45 as poor. Factor loadings of less than or equal to 0.35 are generally considered to be very poor for the purpose of identification and interpretation of factors. Therefore, only those tests which have loadings of more than 0.35 were listed in Table 5.1 to 5.7. Thurstone (1938) too did not regard a projection significant for naming a factor unless it was as large as 0.40 and probably as large as 0.50 or 0.60 to name with confidence, so that the factor accounted for a fourth or third of the variance of a test (Thurstone, 2nd Impression, 1957, p.79).

Factor-A

Table 5.1 snows significant factor loadings of different tests on Factor-A. Out of thirty-seven tests used for this investigation, twenty-four had their significant loadings on Factor-A. Of these twenty-four, twelve had significant loadings on this factor alone; five had their highest (marker) loadings on it while seven had secondary loadings.

TABLE 5.1: Tests High on Varimax Factor-A (Heterogeneous Sample)

Sl. No.	SOI Factor	Name of the Test	Loadings
02	CMU	Word Substitution	0.74**
01	CMU	Verbal Comprehension	0.73**
03	CMU	Word Meaning	0.68*
23	NMC	Word Grouping	0.63*
20	NMU	Word Group Naming	0.61**
07	CMR	Verbal Analogies	0.61**
29	NMS	Sentence Order	0.58**
35	NMI	Syllogisms-III	0.58**
09	CMR	Word Matrix-I	0.55**
04	CMC	Word Classification	0.53**
08	CMR	Word Linkage	0.51**
27	NMR	Inventive Verbal Relations	0.48
31	NMS	Word Matrix-II	0.46**
12	CMS	Necessary Facts	0.45*
28	NMR	Association-IV	0.44
19	CMI	Pertinent Questions	0.44**
26	NMR	Verbal Relations Naming	0.44*
17	CMI	Effects Test	0.44*
15	CMT	Social Institutions	0.41
10	CMS	Necessary Arithmetic Operations	0.40
24	NMC	Group Classification	0.39
06	CMC	Sentence Classification	0.37**
18	CMI	Seeing Problems	0.37
21	NMU	Naming Meaningful Trends	0.36

** Best market (defining) test having significant loading on Factor-A alone.
 * Market test having highest loadings on Factor-A.

A perusal of the above table revealed that twelve tests emerged as relatively pure measures and best markers of Factor-A. Of these twelve tests, ten had fair to excellent sized loadings while two, Pertinent Questions Test and Sentence Classification Test had poor sized loadings. Therefore, they both were considered of little relevance to interpret Factor-A and remaining ten were used to define it. Of the ten defining tests, six, Word Substitution Test, Verbal Comprehension Test, Verbal Analogies Test, Word Matrix-I Test, Word Classification Test and Word Linkage Test were presumed to involve mental operation of cognition according to SOI theory; While remaining four, i.e., Word Group Naming Test, Sentence Order Test, Syllogisms-III Test and Word Matrix-II Test were presumed to involve mental operation of convergent production. Thus, Factor-A had defining loadings on both type of tests, i.e., those presumed to involve the mental operation of cognition and those presumed to involve the mental operation of convergent production. This would suggest a mixed mental operation which is involved in making an inference. This would be so in a situation wherein quite a substantial number of subjects had to go back and forth for cognition of some significant facets of verbal (semantic) fundaments (induction) in order to arrive at the correct response or responses (deduction). For example, in item-3 of the leading defining test, Word Substitution which had excellent sized loading on Factor-A, an examinee had first to discover or identify (cognition) a word out of the four given words similar in meaning to the underlined word in the given sentence. Now, apart from the correct word, the other three words given in alternatives 1, 2 and 4 were very much similar in meaning to the underlined word. Therefore, it may well be that in some of the cases the examinee had to see the context in which the underlined word in the sentence was used to arrive at, identify or choose one unique word (alternative) which would be an appropriate (convergent production) substitute. In the second leading defining test, Verbal Comprehension, which required an examinee to choose one synonym for a verbal concept to identify (cognition) the most appropriate word out of five words of similar meanings, some examinees had to take recourse to cognition as well as convergent production. On the other hand, Word Group Naming Test, which was also a defining test with good sized loading, was a test of convergent production of units according to SOI theory. For example, item Nos. 23, 24 and 27 of it, had elements representing various kinds of musical instruments. The examinee had to put these instruments into an appropriate verbal-concept category (convergent production). To do this, an examinee not only had to identify a characteristic common to all the five elements, but also to identify one functional value (cognition) on the basis of which elements of item No. 23 can be put in the category of wind instruments, elements of item No. 24 as percussion (rhythm) instruments and elements of item No. 27 as string instruments. Similarly, other defining tests may as well be justified to have predisposed a substantial number of subjects to use a mixed mental operation of cognition as well as convergent production.

The marker tests, Word Meaning and Word Grouping, both had very good sized loadings on Factor-A. The secondary loadings of these tests on Factor-B and Factor-C respectively, were almost poor. Hence, they were also considered useful in identifying Factor-A. World Meaning Test was presumed to involve the mental operation of cognition according to SOI theory. One can discover (cognize) a large number of words similar in meaning to each word given in its items, but he may well go back and forth to find out one unique word most appropriate in meaning (convergent production) to the given word. Therefore, this test also predisposed a substantial number of subjects to use a mixed mental operation of cognition as well as of convergent production. Similar was the case with the marker test Word Grouping, which was presumed to involve the mental operation of convergent production according to SOI theory. As in each item of this test also, the examinees may well go back and forth to identify words similar in meaning out of the ten given words (cognition), in order to form four groups of words similar in meaning which could be put into appropriate or acceptable (convergent production) groups. Other marker tests did not appear to be very useful for identifying the nature of Factor-A as they had exactly fair to less than fair-sized loadings on it. Thus, all the marker (including defining) tests having better than fair-sized loadings on Factor-A, whether they involved mental operation of cognition or mental operation of convergent production according to SOI theory, appeared to require at least in case of a substantial number of subjects belonging to heterogeneous sample both the operations alternately in order to perform the semantic task set for them in the various test-questions. Factor-A, therefore, may be identified as representing a mixed mental operation of cognition as well as convergent production which for the sake of convenience can be termed as 'inference'.

Further, out of the ten defining tests (as discussed earlier), three, viz., Word Substitution Test, Verbal Comprehension Test and Word Group Naming Test were presumed to involve SOI's product category of units; one, Word Classification Test was presumed to involve the product category of classes; three, viz., Verbal Analogies Test, Word Matrix-I Test and Word Linkage Test were presumed to involve the product category of relations; two, viz., Sentence Order Test and Word Matrix II test were presumed to involve the product category of systems; one, Syllogisms-III Test was presumed to involve the product category of implications. Out of the five marker tests, two, viz., Word Meaning Test and Word Grouping Test were presumed to involve SOI's product categories of units and classes respectively; while remaining three, viz., Necessary Facts Test, Verbal Relations Naming Test and Effects Test (as discussed earlier) were of little relevance. However, almost all types of tests, i.e., involving SOI's product categories of units, classes, relations, systems and implications (except transformations) were loaded as marker or defining tests with fair to excellent sized loadings on Factor-A. Therefore, Factor-A may be identified as *General Inference of Semantic Products.*

A factor, General Reasoning was repeatedly identified in some of the studies on 'reasoning' conducted earlier but the nature of that factor was entirely different from Factor-A identified in the present study. The General Reasoning Factor identified in those studies was mainly loaded on Arithmetic Reasoning Problem tests (Green *et al.*, 1954; Kettner *et al.*, 1956; Kettner *et al.*, 1959). Bala (1977) also identified a similar factor: Inference or General Cognition and Convergent Production at all the three age levels, 13+, 14+ and 15+ in her study. Logical Classification Test, Apparatus Test, Figure Concepts Test and Missing Links Test which did not find their loadings on Bala's factor at any of the three age levels, did not emerge with significant loading on Factor-A identified in the present study as well. Moreover, Sequential Association Test which had significant loadings on Bala's factor at all the three age levels, did not emerge with significant loading on Factor-A in the present study. Chhikara (1982) also identified a factor: General Cognition and Convergent Production in his study. All the tests except Logical Classification which found loadings on Chhikara's factor, emerged with significant loadings on Factor-A in the present study as well.

Factor-B

Table 5.2 shows significant factor loadings of different tests on Factor-B. Out of thirteen tests which emerged with significant loadings on it, four did not have significant loadings on any other factor; five had their highest loadings while four had only secondary loadings on it.

Out of the four best marker tests which also had fair to very good sized loadings on Factor-B and thus could be considered to define it, two, viz., Ship Destination Test and Different Meanings Test were presumed to involve the mental operation of cognition while the other two, Object Synthesis Test and Missing Links Test were presumed to involve the mental operation of convergent production according to SOI theory. This again, suggested that quite a few subjects adopted a mixed mental operation in making an inference, wherein one has to go back and forth for cognition of significant characteristics of verbal (semantic) fundaments (induction) for arriving at a required response

TABLE 5.2: Tests High on Varimax Factor-B (Heterogeneous Sample)

S. No.	SOI Factor	Name of the Test	Loadings
34	NMT	Object Synthesis	0.63**
33	NMT	Unusual Uses	0.61*
11	CMS	Ship Destination	0.54**
15	CMT	Social Institutions	0.53*
36	NMI	Missing Links	0.51**
27	NMR	Inventive Verbal Relations	0.50*
14	CMT	Different Meanings	0.47**
28	NMR	Association-IV	0.47*
10	CMS	Necessary Arithmetic Operations	0.42*
22	NMU	Picture Group Naming	0.41
12	CMS	Necessary Facts	0.38
03	CMU	Word Meaning	0.38
26	NMR	Verbal Relations Naming	0.38

** Best marker (defining) tests having significant loadings on Factor-B alone
* Marker tests having highest loading on Factor-B.

or responses (deduction). For example, in item No. 1 and other items of the leading defining test Object Synthesis, an examinee was required to make an appropriate object (convergent production) out of the two given objects. To do this, he may well go back and forth in finding or discovering what objects he could make of those objects (cognition), like, paper bag, kite, paper ball, toy, a number of patterns or designs etc, out of which he could then select the most appropriate one (convergent production). On the other hand, in the next defining test Ship Destination, an examinee was required to discover shortest routes from ships to ports (cognition) under the constraints of several variables. But as may be seen in item No. 1 and other items, the examinee may well discover many routes to choose from, in order to arrive at or identify which would be the shortest (convergent production). Thus, this test could also be presumed to involve a mixed mental operation of cognition as well as convergent production. Similar could be the case with the other two defining tests, Missing Links and Different Meanings. In Missing Links Test, an examinee could well begin by taking into cognition three verbal concepts (fundaments) in between two verbal concepts in order to form an acceptable chain of association (convergent production). In Different Meaning Test, he could identify four verbal concepts for a given verbal concept, which could be of use in different situations (cognition), but to arrive at such verbal concepts some may well have to check the accepted meanings of the given verbal concept specific to the different situations (convergent production),

Amongst the five marker tests, Unusual Uses Test had the highest and good sized loading on Factor-B. It had poor sized loading on Factor-E as well which will be discussed later. Therefore, it could also be considered for identifying the nature of Factor-B. In each item of this test, an examinee was asked to write an unusual use of an object or element whose common use was already mentioned. One may well discover a large number of uses of an object (cognition) out of which he could then pick up that one which would be most uncommon though appropriate (convergent production). Thus, Unusual Uses Test also involved mixed mental operation of convergent production as well as cognition. Similar was the case with the other two marker tests, Social Institutions and Association-IV which have fair sized loadings on Factor-B but poor sized loadings on Factor-A. In Social Institutions Test an examinee may well discover a larger number of improvements (cognition) in the given social institutions, out of which he could then pick up two which would be most appropriate and definite (convergent production). In Association-IV Test, he may well discover a large number of words (fundaments) related with the given (two) verbal concepts (cognition), out of which he could then pick up one which would be most appropriately though differently (convergent production) related with them. The marker test Inventive Verbal Relations had fair sized loading on Factor-B and same sized loadings on Factor-A discussed earlier. Thus, being a complex variable, it was considered to be of little relevance for interpreting Factor-B. However, as Factor-A has already been identified as involving mixed mental operation of cognition as well as convergent production and other tests which have fair to very good sized loadings on Factor-B have already been justified to involve a mixed mental operation of convergent production as well as cognition, the presence of Inventive Verbal Relation Test on Factor-B needs no consideration. The marker test Necessary Arithmetic Operation had poor sized loading on Factor-B. Therefore, it was of little relevance for interpreting Factor-B.

Given that all the defining and marker variables which have fair to very good sized loadings on Factor-B, involved a mixed mental operation of cognition as well as convergent production at least in case of a substantial number of subjects belonging to heterogeneous sample, which for the sake of convenience may be identified as 'inference'.

Further, as far as SOI's product categories were concerned, out of the four defining tests, two, viz., Object Synthesis Test and Different Meanings Test, were presumed to involve product category of transformation, while the remaining two, i.e., Ship Destination Test and Missing Links Test were presumed to involve the product categories of systems and implications respectively. But, as all these test having better than fair sized loadings, were relatively pure measures of Factor-B, they should share the same product of information in common to emerge together on it. A perusal of the nature of these tests revealed that they all required inferring such items of information which were in a way 'mutations' of the given information. For example, in Object Synthesis Test, the examinees in each item while producing an object out of the two given objects had to modify, revise or mutate their earlier conception, so as to use them (by combining) in an unique but different way. Similarly, in each item of Different Meanings Test, they had to revise the meaning of the given verbal concept after each attempt, to find four verbal concepts as meanings of the given verbal concept which could be appropriate for use in different situations.

Thus, both these tests involved 'mutations'. Even otherwise, both these tests were presumed to involve SOI's product category of transformations, which may be termed as mutations. The term 'mutations' appeared to be appropriate not only to differentiate it from Guilford's product terminology, but also, because it appeared to be a more inclusive concept, as it involves change in form, nature, qualities, modification, variety, difference, departure, unlikeness, category, classification, similarly (*Webster's New World Thesaurus*, Simson and Schustler, 1971). Similarly, in each item of the Ship Destination Test, the examinees were required to find out the shortest route from ship to port which had to be seen by them as a modified course under the influence of wind direction and/or sea waves. For example, in its item No. 1, the examinees were asked to find out the shortest distance from Ship-A to Port-B, which was two km. Because the wind was blowing in the same direction as the course of Ship A to Port B, it had reduced its distance by one km. So also, was the case with its other items. Thus, change in the original information or 'mutuations' of information was involved in Ship Destination Test also. Similar was the case with the defining test Missing Links which required the examinees to find out three verbal concepts in between two given verbal concepts, different in meanings but each related to its preceding one so as to form a chain of association. For example, in its example No. 1, the first word was written as 'red' and the last one as 'ice'. The inferred word 'sun' was stated to be related to the word 'red' because 'sun' being red in the morning and in the evening. The next inferred word 'weather' was stated to be related to the word 'sun', because it is being controlled by the sun. The last inferred word 'cold' was stated to be related to the word 'weather' and 'ice' because weather could be cold, but ice being cold always. Thus a chain of association was formed which began with the word 'red' and ended with the word 'ice', and in this chain each word was related to its immediate preceding one and there could be other chains as well. Thus, it involved seeing the fundaments related in a different way. Similar was the case with other items of the Missing Links Test. Thus, all the defining tests for Factor-B, involved product of information of 'mutation'.

Out of the five marker variables, two, viz., Unusual Uses Test and Social Institutions Test were presumed to involve SOI's product category of transformations which has already been subsumed under 'mutations'. The marker test Association-IV was presumed to involve the product category of relations, but it, too, involved seeing a fundament in each item which was related differently (mutations) with the two given fundaments. The marker test Inventive Verbal Relations as discussed earlier, was a complex one, but it too, involved seeing the verbal fundaments related in different ways with the given verbal fundaments in substantial number of its items. The marker test Necessary Arithmetic Operations as discussed earlier, was of little relevance.

Given the semantic information in the test-tasks of the defining and marker tests, Object Synthesis, Ship Destination, Missing Links, Different Meanings, Unusual Uses, Social Institutions, Association-IV and Inventive Verbal Relations with the mixed mental operation of cognition as well as convergent production, the products then are those of mutations. Factor-B can therefore be identified *Inference of Semantic Mutations.*

Factor-C

Table 5.3 shows significant factor loadings of five tests on Factor-C. Two of these tests had significant loadings on Factor-C alone while one had its highest and two others had secondary loadings on it.

TABLE 5.3: Tests High on Varimax Factor-C (Heterogeneous Sample)

S. No.	SOI Factor	Name of the Test	Loadings
30	NMS	Temporal Order	0.58**
32	NMT	Gestalt Transformation	0.57**
24	NMC	Group Classification	0.57*
23	NMC	Word Grouping	0.43
18	CMI	Seeing Problems	0.37

** Best marker (defining) test having significant loadings on Factor-C alone.
* Marker tests having highest loading on Factor-C.

The best marker tests for Factor-C were Temporal Order and Gestalt Transformations. As they both had good sized loadings, therefore, they both could be used to define Factor-C. The marker test Group Classification also had good sized loading on Factor-C. As it had poor sized loadings on Factor-A and Factor-G (to be discussed later), it could also be considered to interpret Factor-C. World Grouping Test and Seeing Problems Test had poor sized secondary loadings. Therefore, they were of little relevance for interpreting Factor-C. In Temporal Order Test necessary steps to accomplish different tasks were given in scrambled order. Three questions were given below each task. In order to answer those questions, an examinee had to arrange the given (verbally described) steps into an appropriate meaningful order (convergent production). Similarly, in each item of Gestalt Transformation Test. A task, below which were given four objects, was given to the examinees. The task in question could be accomplished by any one of those four objects or part thereof or by none of the given objects. The examinees were required to find out which of of those objects or part thereof, or none of the objects was appropriate (convergent production) to accomplish it. Thus, both Temporal Order Test and Gestalt Transformation Test involved mental operation of Convergent production. Next, in each item of the marker test, Group Classification two 'target groups' of three different verbal lables or three words-each defining a class, were given. Below these 'target groups' were given eight word sets of three words each. An examinee in each item of this test was asked to choose four (related) words each from a different word set such that those words could be appropriately classed with (convergent production) one of the (class) words in any of the two 'target groups'. So, Group Classification Test also involved mental operation of convergent production. Factor-C may, therefore, be identified as involving the mental operation of 'convergent production'.

Further, Temporal Order Test was presumed to involve SOI's product category of systems, Gestalt Transformation Test the product category of transformations and Group Classification test the product category of classes. However, as all these tests had good sized loadings on Factor-C, it suggested that they had in common the same product of information to emerge together. A perusal of the nature of all these tests revealed that they involved processing of the given items of information to arrive at some desired 'formations'. As in each item of Temporal Order the examinees were asked to form a correct or meaningful order out of the verbally described scrambled steps. In Gestalt Transformation Test they were asked to choose an object out of the four given objects for use in an unusual form. In Group Classification Test they were asked to form two groups of four words each from the given sets of three words each. Thus, all these tests were concerned with a mixed product dimension 'formations'.

Given the semantic information in the test-task of defining and marker tests, Temporal Order, Gestalt Transformations and Group Classification with the mental operation of convergent production, the products then are those of 'formations'. Factor-C can, therefore, be identified as *Convergent Production of Semantic Formations.*

Factor-D

Table 5.4 given below shows significant factor loading of only one test on Factor-D, as no other test could emerge with significant loading on it. Also this test did not have its significant loading on any other factor; so it emerged as its sole defining test.

TABLE 5.4: Tests High on Varimax Factor-D (Heterogeneous Sample)

S. No.	SOI Factor	Name of the Test	Loadings
05	CMC	Logical Classification	0.68**

** Best marker (defining) test having significant loadings on Factor-D alone.

Logical Classification Test was the single best marker test for Factor-D having very good sized loading. Therefore, Factor-D was a singlet which was determined by Logical Classification Test only. In each item of Local Classification Test a verbal (semantic) statement and four verbal concepts defining four different classes were given. The examinees were asked to classify the given statement into one of the four given classes, for which he had to identify the significant characteristic of the given verbal statement (cognition). After obtaining this information which was contained in the given statement itself, he would classify the given statement into one of the four verbal concepts. Therefore, Logical Classification Test involved mental operation of cognition and product category of classes. According to SOI theory also, Logical Classification Test was presumed to involve the mental operation of cognition and product category of classes. Therefore, Factor-D can therefore be identified as *Cognition of Semantic Classes.*

Factor-E

Table 5.5 given below shows significant factor loadings of only seven tests on Factor-E. Out of the seven tests, two had their significant loadings on Factor-E alone while three had their highest loadings and two had their secondary loadings on it.

TABLE 5.5: Tests High on Varimax Factor-E (Heterogeneous Sample)

S. No.	SOI Factor	Name of the Test	Loadings
13	CMT	Similarities	0.68**
25	NMC	Figure Concepts	0.60**
21	NMU	Naming Meaningful Trends	0.55*
33	NMT	Unusual Uses	0.44
18	CMI	Seeing Problems	0.43*
22	NMU	Picture Group Naming	0.42*
17	CMI	Effects Test	0.37

** Best marker (defining) test having significant loadings on Factor-E alone.
* Market test having highest loadings on Factor-E.

Similarities Test and Figure concepts Test were the two best marker variables for Factor-E. As they had good to very good sized loadings, they could be used to define it. Similarities Test was presumed to involve the mental operation of cognition while Figure Concepts Test was presumed to involve the mental operation of convergent production. So, Factor-E had defining loadings on both type of tests, i.e., those involving mental operation of cognition and mental operation of convergent production. This would suggest a mixed mental operation which is involved in making inferences wherein one had to go back and forth for cognition of significant characteristics of the given fundaments in terms of their form, utility, use or other qualities (induction) to arrive at the correct response or responses (deduction). As in each item of Similarities Test, two objects were given. One may well go back and forth to look for the characteristics similar in form, utility, use, shape or other qualities (cognition) between those objects on the basis of which those objects could be appropriately put into acceptable groups/classes or categories (convergent production). For example, in question No. 5 of this test, a bullock cart and a motor-bus were given. The examinees had to first look for the various characteristics similar to both these objects (cognition) and then to find out which three of them were the most appropriate on the basis of which a bullock cart and a motor but could be put into acceptable groups (convergent production), viz., both have wheels; both are used for transportation; both are driven by men. Likewise, in Figure Concepts Test, line drawings of twenty different objects were given. The examinees may well go back and forth in order to identify the characteristics or properties common to any two of those objects (cognition) so as to name the acceptable verbal concept under which those could be appropriately grouped together (convergent production). For instance, the example given in this test had line drawings of six different objects – an owl, chicks, a baby, a deer, a shoe and a parrot. The examinees could adopt various strategies to identify the characteristics common to any two of these objects. One might identify an owl as a 'living being' (cognition). He would then look for this characteristic in any of the other five fundaments and by successive scanning establish this connection of 'living things' between the first object (owl) and the second object (chicks), and thus deduce the other to be an instance of this connection (convergent production). Or, he may look for connections amongst objects (cognition) by simultaneous scanning or by conservative focussing or foçuss gambling and arrive at appropriate acceptable connections to produce a verbal concept and its instances (convergent production), like, 'living things' in case of owl and chicks; also 'flying animals' in case of owl and chicks; 'childhood' in case of chicks and baby etc.

Out of the three marker test only one, i.e., Naming Meaningful Trends Test had good sized loadings on Factor-E (and poor sized loading on Factor-A) while other two, i.e., Seeing Problems Test and Picture Group Naming Test had poor sized loadings. Therefore, they were considered to be of little relevance for interpreting Factor-E and only Naming Meaningful Trend Test could be considered to interpret it. Naming Meaningful Trend was presumed to involve the mental operation of convergent production according to SOI theory. However, its good sized loading together with defining tests. Similarities and Figure concepts, suggested that it predisposed a substantial number of subjects to use a mixed mental operation of cognition as well as convergent production. For example, in item No. 4 of this test, six verbal (semantic) fundaments, like, an infant, a child, an adolescent, a youth, an adult and an aged (old) were given. An examinee may well look for connections amongst these fundaments (cognition) and by simultaneous scanning or by conservative focussing may arrive at an appropriate acceptable verbal concept, 'increasing age' which would describe an ordered connection between these fundaments (convergent production). Thus, both the defining tests. Similarities and Figure Concepts as well as the marker test Naming Meaningful Trends involved mixed mental operation of cognition as well as convergent production at least in case of substantial number of subjects belonging to heterogeneous sample, Factor-E may therefore be identified for the sake of convenience as involving mental operation of 'inference'.

Further, Similarities Test was presumed to involve SOI's product category of transformations, Figure Concept Test the product category of classes and Naming Meaningful Trend Test the product category of units. However, as all these tests had good to very good sized loadings on Factor-E, it suggested that they had in common the same product of information to emerge together. A perusal of the nature of these tests revealed that they all entailed establishing connections between or amongst the common attributes or properties of objects or events. For example, in case of Similarities Test the examinees were given two objects and after identifying their attributes, had to infer such connections in the attributes that the objects could be put together in three different groups. In Figure Concepts Test, they had to establish connections between any two of the line drawings in terms of their common characteristics or properties. In Naming Meaningful Trends Test they had to establish connections between the given verbal (semantic) fundaments in order to name the trend.

Given the semantic information in test-tasks of defining and marker tests, Similarities, Figure Concepts and Naming Meaningful Trends with the mixed mental operation of cognition as well as convergent production, the products then are those of connections. Factor-E can therefore be identified as *Inference of Semantic Connections*.

Factor-F

Table 5.6 given below shows factor loading of only one test on Factor-F, as none of the other tests used for the present investigation could emerge with significant loadings on it. Also, this test did not have its significant loading on any other factor.

TABLE 5.6: Tests High on Varimax Factor-F (Heterogeneous Sample)

S. No.	SOI Factor	Name of the Test	Loadings
16	CMI	Apparatus Test	0.78**

** Best marker (defining) test having significant loadings on Factor-F alone.

Apparatus Test was the only test which emerged as a defining test with excellent sized loading on Factor-F. Therefore, Factor-F was a singlet which was determined by Apparatus Test only. In each item of this test a familiar appliance was given. The examinees were asked to suggest two improvements in each of those appliances. It involved fore-sight in seeing deficiencies, difficulties or defects with respect to the meaningful events connected with the given appliances and thus cognition of semantic implications. According to SOI theory also, Apparatus Test was presumed to involve the mental operation of cognition and product category of implications. Therefore, Factor-F of which Apparatus Test was a single determiner, may be identified as *Cognition of Semantic Implications.*

A similar factor, 'Conceptual Foresight or Cognition of Semantic Implications' was also identified in the study undertaken by Bala (1977) with Apparatus Test having just good sized (oblique) loading. In Chhikara's (1982) study, Apparatus Test emerged on a mixed factor, 'Eduction of Relations and Implications' with excellent sized (Varimax) loading. A similar factor, 'Cognition of Semantic Implications' with Apparatus Test as the leading defining variable having excellent sized (varimax) loading, was also identified in Tewari's (1985) Study. A factor, 'Cognition of Semantic Implications' was also identified by Singh (1987). Apparatus Test, However, emerged on mixed factors, 'Eduction of Categories and Implications' with very good sized (varimax) loading, and on *Deduction of Categories and Implications* with poor sized (though significant) (varimax) loading in Singh's study.

Factor-G

Table 5.7 given below shows significant loadings of only two tests on Factor-G, as none of the other tests used for the present study could emerge with significant loadings on it. Of these two tests, one had its significant loading on Factor-G alone while another had secondary loading.

TABLE 5.7: Tests High on Varimax Factor-G (Heterogeneous Sample)

S. No.	SOI Factor	Name of the Test	Loadings
37	NMI	Sequential Association	0.78**
24	NMC	Group Classification	0.37

** Best marker (defining) test having significant loadings on Factor-G alone.

Sequential Association Test was the single best marker (defining) test for Factor-G. At it had an excellent sized loading and no other marker test was loaded on Factor-G. Factor-G was therefore determined by Sequential Association Test only. In each item of Sequential Association Test four verbal concepts (fundaments) were given to the examinees and they were asked to put them in a sequence, keeping in view the natural connection from first to second verbal concept, second to third verbal concept, and so on. As the order of verbal concepts was of a sufficiently determined order, so the mental operation involved to arrive at the correct sequence was a convergent one. Further, as each verbal concept best implied the one that followed it, so the product of information was in terms of 'implications'. Factor-G may therefore be identified as *Convergent Production of Semantic Implications.* As Group Classification Test had poor sized secondary loading, it was considered of little relevance for interpreting Factor-G.

A similar factor 'Deduction of Inferences or Convergent Production of Semantic Implications' with Sequential Association Test as the leading defining variable and as the sole determiner, was also identified by Chhikara (1982) and Tewari (1985) respectively.

Results for the Homogeneous Samples

The eigen values in descending order of magnitude for the complete correlation matrix (with diagonal entries one) for the homogeneous sample are given in Table IV, Appendix D. It was observed from this table that out of thirty-seven, only eleven ėigen values were greater than one. It suggested that the number of factors necessary to describe the total communality among the thirty-seven variables in case of homogeneous sample must be upto eleven. As earlier, the communality for each of the thirty-seven variables was then estimated from the first eleven principal axes. These estimated communalities were placed in the diagonal cells of the correlation matrix for the homogeneous sample given in Appendix C. The correlation matrix so obtained was then factor analyzed to get the first eleven principal factors. The eleven factors so obtained and estimated communality for each of the thirty-seven variables are given in Table V, Appendix D. It (Table V) revealed that almost all the variables had negative loadings on Factor-1, and roughly half of the variables had positive and half of the variables negative loadings on other factors. Besides, each variable had loadings on more than one factor. This made interpretation of factors difficult. As discussed earlier, the factors were therefore, rotated to obtain varimax orthogonal factors to facilitate their interpretation. The varimax orthogonal rotated factors for the homogeneous sample are given in Table VI, Appendix D.

The very first thing which struck the author when taking up the interpretation of the varimax rotated factors for the homogeneous sample was the fact that while the heterogeneous sample provided seven factors, the homogeneous sample drawn from it provided eleven factors. Out of these eleven factors, one factor – Factor-11, of the homogeneous sample, was identical with Factor-7 of the heterogeneous sample; while rest of the factor of the homogeneous sample appeared to be differentiated independent factors of the factors in the heterogeneous sample.

So far, going by the generally accepted criterion of a loading of 0.35 of any test on any factor for interpretative purposes, various tests which had such loadings on different factors were taken up. But for interpretation of the homogeneous sample factors, considering the suggestion of Comrey (1973, p.226) that, "Commonsense dictates that factor interpretation based on a few variables with only poor to fair rating . . . must be made very cautiously and with every expectation that substantial revisions may be necessary in the future". Thus the criterion of a loading of 0.35 and above had to be re-evaluated. For, what this suggestion amounted to, was that the loadings of 0.45 and below were of little consequence, specially, in case of such factors, wherein tests of good (0.55) to excellent (0.71) loadings were available. As pointed by Comrey *(Ibid.)* again, "If several data variables are available with loadings in the very good to excellent category, the investigator can afford to be somewhat more definite". Taking cue from this and considering again the fact that all the eleven factors of homogenous group had tests having good to excellent size loadings, the investigator decided not to pay too much attention to such tests which had loadings less than or equal to 0.45 for interpretation purposes.

Not is this all, Comrey (1973, pp.226-227) points out:

> Factor interpretation ideally should go beyond merely determining which data variables are like the factor and which are not and the resultant identification and naming of what appears to be the common element or elements represented by the factor. The best kind of factor interpretation will also shed some light on several other areas of concern. Where does this factor lie in the hierarchy of factors? It is a relatively specific level factor that is too limited in scope to be of much scientific value or is it very broad and complex, perhaps, too much so? . . . What potential value does the factor have for purposes of general scientific description and theory building?

Taking cue from Comrey for identifying potential value of the factor loadings of a test for the purposes of placement on a factor which could help in description and theory building, the present investigator had to make a choice in case of tests with substantial loadings in one of the factor in the homogeneous sample while the same test or tests had significant loadings on two or three factors in the heterogeneous sample. As most of such tests contributed to the identification of mixed factors in case of heterogeneous sample which did not relate to previously developed SOI factors, author chose to interpret such tests on the basis of common element or elements, with differentiated independent factors of the homogeneous sample.

A grid was prepared for this purpose by placing the tests of factors in the heterogeneous sample in the rows and that of factors in the homogeneous sample in the columns. On the basis of the criteria discussed earlier, only those tests were listed which had substantial loadings in case of both the factors. Thus, four patterns as given below emerged:

1. Identical Factor (IF) – a factor which had identical tests in both the samples and therefore had no problem for its interpretation.
2. Differentiated Independent Factors (DF) – factors of the heterogeneous sample which had defining tests in one factor or more than one factor in case of the homogeneous sample.
3. Tests with substantial loadings (T) – tests with substantial loadings on a factor of the homogeneous sample which could be interpreted together with the differentiated factors (DF) on the basis of common elements.
4. Tests with poor loadings (P) – tests on a factor of homogeneous sample which were of little consequence to identify differentiated factor (DF).

Table 5.8 shows the overlapping among the factors in the homogeneous and heterogeneous samples.

TABLE 5.8: Overlapping among factors in the Heterogeneous and Homogeneous Samples

Heterogeneous Sample Factors	Homogeneous Sample Factors 1	2	3	4	5	6	7	8	9	10	11
A	DF	P		DF	T		P		P		
B		DF	T		T	P		P		DF	
C						DF	DF				
D									DF		
E				T	DF		P	DF			
F			DF								
G											IF

IF Identical Factor.
DF Differentiated independent factor in the homogeneous sample.
T Factor having test with substantial loading which could be interpreted with differentiated independent factor (DF) on the basis of common elements
P Factors having tests with poor loadings.

As is indicated by the above table, seventeen tests which had marker loadings on Factor-A in the heterogeneous sample, emerged with significant loadings in six different factors in the homogeneous sample. Out of those six factors, three factors – Factor-2, 7 and 9, had tests with poor sized loadings; so were of little interpretative value. One factor – Factor-5, had a test with substantial loadings, but that was such which could be interpreted with the differentiated factor of Factor-E of heterogeneous sample, on account of common elements, the remaining two factors – Factor-12 and Factor-4, had most of the marker tests in common with Factor-A. Thus they could well be identified as the differentiated factors of it.

Nine tests which had marker loadings on Factor-B in the heterogeneous sample were distributed on six factors in the homogeneous sample. Two of these factors – Factor-6 and Factor-8, had tests with poor loadings on them; thus, they were of little interpretative value. Two factors – Factor-3 and 5, had tests with substantial loadings, but they were such that could be interpreted with the differentiated factors of Factor-F and Factor-E respectively, on account of common elements. The remaining two factors – Factor-2 and Factor-10, could be identified as differentiated factors of Factor-B of the heterogeneous sample; as some tests in case of Factor-2 had poor loadings on Factor-A and none of tests in case of Factor 10 had their loadings in any other factor of the heterogeneous sample.

Three tests with marker loadings on Factor-C in the heterogeneous sample were divided into two factors – Factor-6 and Factor-7 in the homogenous sample. These tests emerged as defining tests with substantial loadings on these factors. Factor-6 and Factor-7 could, therefore, be identified as differentiated factors of Factor-C.

Factor-D in the heterogeneous sample was a signlet factor which had an overlap with Factor-9 in the homogeneous sample, though some of the variables of Factor-9 shared poor inconsequential loadings with Factor-A of the heterogeneous sample.

Five marker (including defining) tests of Factor-E in the heterogeneous sample were divided on four factors – Factor-4, Factor-5, Factor-7 and Factor-8, in the homogeneous sample. As one of these tests, which emerged on Factor-7 in the homogeneous sample had poor sized loading on Factor-E itself; hence, Factor-7 of the homogenous sample could not be treated as a differentiated factor of Factor-E of the heterogeneous sample. Factor-4 had a test with substantial loading on Factor-E but it had to be interpreted with the differentiated factors of Factor-A of the heterogeneous sample, on account of common elements. Factor-5 and Factor-8 could, therefore, be identified as differentiated factors of Factor-E.

Factor-F in the heterogeneous sample had its sole determining test with substantial loading overlapping in the tests of Factor-3 of the homogeneous sample which in turn had another test with substantial loading on it, but fair sized loading on Factor-B of heterogeneous sample. As there were common elements in terms of product implications, and as the common tests of Factor-F of heterogeneous sample and Factor-3 of homogeneous sample had very excellent loadings, Factor-3 could, therefore, be treated as the differentiated factor of Factor-F.

Both factors – Factor-G in the heterogeneous sample and Factor-11 in the homogeneous, sample were signlets which were identical.

Thus, out of seven factors which emerged in the heterogeneous sample, six differentiated into ten independent factors in the homogeneous sample and one factor emerged identical in both the samples.

Next, an attempt was made to interpret each of these ten differentiated independent factors in the homogeneous sample. The order of interpretation was decided according to the order of the factors in the heterogeneous sample and their placement in those factors. For the sake of convenience, a differentiated independent factor in the homogeneous sample was identified with the same alphabet as of the factor in the heterogeneous sample but followed by a letter 'M' to indicate it to be a factor in the homogeneous sample. The subscript after letter 'M' indicated the order of the factor in the homogeneous sample. Thus, starting with Factor-A of the heterogeneous sample, its two differentiated factors in the homogeneous sample were denoted by Factor-AM_1 and Factor-AM_4; the two differentiated factors of Factor-B were indicated by Factor-BM_2 and Factor-BM_{10}; the two differentiated factors of Factor-C were indicated by Factor-CM_6 and Factor-CM_7; the differentiated factor of Factor-D was indicated by Factor-DM_9; two differentiated factors of Factor-E were indicated by Factor-EM_5 and Factor-EM_8; the differentiated factor of Factor-F was indicated by Factor-FM_3; finally, the identical factor of Factor-G was indicated by Factor-GM_{11} for further discussion. Each of these differentiated factors have been discussed in turn in the following sections. Tables 5.9 to 5.19 have been gleaned from Table-VI, Appendix-D.

Factor-AM_1

Table 5.9 shows the test with significant loadings on Factor-AM_1 in the homogeneous sample together with their loadings on the factors in the heterogeneous sample. Out of the eight tests which emerged with significant loadings on Factor-AM_1 in the homogeneous sample, seven had defining or marker loadings on Factor-A in the heterogeneous sample, while remaining one, Inventive Verbal Relations Test, though had marker loading on Factor-B of the heterogeneous sample yet it had same sized loading on Factor-A.

TABLE 5.9: Tests High on Varimax Factor-AM_1 in the Homogeneous Sample (together with their Loadings on Heterogeneous Sample Factors)

Sl. No.	SOI	Name of the Test Factor	Loadings	Heterogeneous Sample Factor Loadings		
				A	B	C
01	CMU	Verbal Comprehension	0.76**	0.73**		
02	CMU	Word Substitution	0.74**	0.74**		
03	CMU	Word Meaning	0.62**	0.68*	0.38	
08	CMR	Word Linkage	0.46**	0.51**		
29	NMS	Sentence Order	0.45* (P)	0.58**		
23	NMC	Word Grouping	0.44* (P)	0.63*		0.43
27	NMR	Inventive Verbal	0.41	0.48	50 *	
04	CMC	Word Classification	0.37	0.53**		

** Defining Test.
* Marker Test.
(P) Test with poor loading.

Out of the eight tests which had significant loadings on Factor-AM_1, first four emerged as defining test, next two as marker tests and last two as secondary test. The two marker and two secondary tests had just fair to poor sized loadings on Factor-AM_1. Therefore, they were considered to be of little interpretative value. So, only first four tests could be considered to interpret Factor-AM_1 of the homogeneous sample. These four tests, viz., Verbal Comprehension, Word Substitution, Word Meaning and Word Linkage were presumed to involve the mental operation of cognition according to SOI theory. Because all these test together with some convergent production tests emerged on Factor-A in the heterogeneous sample, it was presumed that they predisposed a substantial number of subjects to use a mixed mental operation of cognition as well as convergent production in the heterogeneous sample. However, as none of the convergent production tests emerged with better than fair sized loading on Factor-AM_1 in the homogeneous sample, so it was presumed that whatever little variance in terms of mental operation of convergent production these tests had in the heterogeneous sample, was of little consequence for interpretation in the homogeneous sample. Therefore, Factor-AM_1 on which all these tests involving mental operation of cognition have emerged together as defining tests, may be identified to involve mental operation of 'cognition'.

Further, all the first three defining tests, Verbal Comprehension. Word Substitution and Word Meaning which had almost very good to excellent sized loadings on Factor-AM_1, were presumed to involve SOI's product category of units. The last defining test, Word Linkage had just fair sized loading; so it could have been ignored but being a defining test, it needed some attention. In Word Linkage Test two verbal concepts which were related though differently to one of the three given words, were given. The examinees were asked to identify that one word which had different relations with those (two) different and unrelated verbal concepts. It appeared that the examinees in this test had adopted a successive scanning strategy by placing one alternative after another in order to see which one of the three given words had different relations with the two verbal concepts. This is to say that each word in Word Linkage Test had been treated as a 'unit', as in case of Word Substitution and Word Meaning tests. Thus it can be presumed that this test, too, had some amount of variance in common with the product dimension of units although it was presumed to involve the product category of 'relations' according to SOI theory.

Given the semantic information in the test tasks of defining tests–Verbal Comprehension, Word Substitution, Word Meaning and Word Linkage with the mental operation of cognition, the products then are those of units. Factor-AM_1 can be identified as *Cognition of Semantic Units*.

Factor-AM_4

Table 5.10 shows the tests with significant loadings on Factor-AM_4 in the homogeneous sample together with their loadings on factors in the heterogeneous sample. Out of the five tests which all emerged as defining tests for Factor-AM_4 in the homogeneous sample, three, viz., Verbal Analogies Test, Syllogisms-III Test and Pertinent Questions Test were defining tests for Factor-A in the heterogeneous sample as well; one, viz., Effect Test was marker test for Factor-A; and one, viz., Figure Concepts Test was defining test for Factor-E in the heterogeneous sample. Figure Concepts Test emerged on Factor-AM_4 with substantial loading which could be due to elements in common with the defining tests – Verbal Analogies, Effect Test and Syllogisms-III.

TABLE 5.10: Tests High on Varimax Factor-AM_4 in the Homogeneous Sample (together with their Loadings on Heterogeneous Sample Factors Loadings)

Sl. No.	SOI	Name of the Test Factor	Loadings	Heterogeneous Sample Factor Loadings	
				A	E
07	CMR	Verbal Analogies	0.67**	0.61**	
25	NMC	Figure Concepts	0.61**(T)		0.60**
17	CMI	Effect Test	0.55**	0.44*	0.37
35	NMI	Syllogism-III	0.52**	0.58**	
19	CMI	Pertinent Questions	0.39**(P)	0.44**	

** Defining Test.
* Marker Test.

Out of all the five defining tests of Factor-AM_4 the last one, i.e., pertinent Questions Test had poor sized loading; so it was considered to be of little consequence to interpret Factor-AM_4. Therefore, only four tests could be considered to interpret it purposefully. Out of these four test two, viz., Verbal Analogies Test and Effect Test were presumed to involve the mental operation of cognition while remaining two, Figure Concepts Test and Syllogisms-III Test were presumed to involve the mental operation of convergent production according to SOI theory. This would suggest a mixed mental operation of cognition as well as convergent production, that is, 'inference' was involved in all these tests. The same was true in case of heterogeneous sample, too, as Factor-A or E on which these tests were loaded as defining or marker tests were found to involve a mixed mental operation 'inference'. Factor-AM_4 may, therefore, be identified as involving the mental operation of 'Inference'.

Further, Verbal Analogies Test was presumed to involve SOI's product category of relations, Figure Concepts Test the product category of classes, both Effect Test and Syllogisms-III Test the product category of implications. However, fair to good sized loadings of these tests on Factor-AM_4 suggested that they shared the same product of information in common to emerge together on it. A perusal of the nature of these tests revealed that an examinee in all these tests had to arrive at the 'referents', from the given items of information. For instance, in case of Verbal Analogies Test an examinee was required to find out a verbal concept out of the four given verbal concept which had same relationship to the verbal concept given to the right of the sign (: :), similar to or as between two verbal concepts to the left of it. Thus, the relationship in each item of this test was specified by two given verbal concepts which served as 'referent'. Similarly, in Figure Concepts Test the common attributes of any two figures out of sixteen figures served as 'referents' for connecting them with each other to form a class. (Figure concepts test was presumed to involve the same mental operation 'inference' but a different product of information connections' in case of Factor-E in the heterogeneous sample. Connection being a much broader term than referents, it was presumed that whatever variance this test had in the product 'connections' in case of the heterogeneous sample, has emerged as the product of information, 'referents' in the homogeneous sample). Similar was the case with Effect Test in which 'present events' served as 'referents' to infer future effects. Similarly, in Syllogisms-III Test the given statements or 'premises' served as 'referents' to infer the outcomes.

Given the semantic information in the test-tasks of all the four defining tests, Verbal Analogies, Figure Concepts, Effects Test and Syllogisms-III with the mixed mental operation of inference, the products then are those of referents. Factor-AM_4 can therefore be identified as *Inference of Semantic Referents.*

Factor-BM_2

Table 5.11 shows the tests with significant loadings on Factor-BM_2 of the homogeneous sample together with their loadings on factors of the heterogeneous sample. Out of the nine marker (including four defining) tests for Factor-B in the heterogeneous sample, two-Association-IV Test and Inventive Verbal Relations Test, emerged with significant loadings on Factor-BM_2 in the homogeneous sample. Another test, verbal Relations Naming which also emerged with significant loadings on Factor-BM_2, had marker though poor sized loading on Factor-A in the heterogeneous sample; yet it had almost same sized loading on Factor-B in the heterogeneous sample. Considering its marker loading though just fair sized on Factor-BM_2 and secondary loading on Factor-EM_5 (to be discussed later on), and the fact that it emerged together with one NMR defining test Association-IV which had an excellent loading on Factor-BM_2, it would be worthwhile to take it up with Factor-BM_2.

TABLE 5.11: Tests High on Varimax Factor-BM_2 in the Homogeneous Sample (together with their Loadings on Heterogeneous Sample Factors)

Sl. No.	SOI	Name of the Test Factor	Loadings	Heterogeneous Sample Factor Loadings	
				A	B
28	NMR	Association-IV	0.83**	0.44	0.47*
26	NMR	Verbal Relations Naming	0.45*(P)	0.44*	0.38
27	NMR	Inventive Verbal Relations	0.42*(P)	0.48	0.50*

** Defining Test.
* Marker Test.

Out of the three tests which had significant loadings on Factor-BM_2, one, Association-IV Test had very excellent sized defining loading, while remaining two, i.e., Verbal Relations Naming Test and Inventive Verbal Relations Test had just fair sized, and poor sized loadings respectively. Thus, though both were of little use to interpret Factor-BM_2 and Association-IV Test with the defining and excellent sized loading would have sufficed to interpret it, yet they were of significance, as both involved the same mental operation of convergent production and same product category of relations of SOI model as Association-IV Test.

Given the semantic information in the test-tasks of the defining test Association-IV, and also in the marker tests, Verbal Relations Naming and Inventive Verbal Relations with the mental operation of convergent production, the products being those of relations, Factor-BM_2 can be identified as *Convergent Production of Semantic Relations.*

A similar factor, 'Deduction of Semantic Relations' with Association-IV test as the leading defining test having a loading of 0.74 (varimax) was also identified by Tyagi (1987).

Factor-BM_{10}

Table 5.12 shows tests with significant loadings on Factor-BM_{10} in the homogeneous sample together with their loadings on factors in the heterogeneous sample. All the four test which emerged with significant loadings on Factor-BM_{10}, had either marker on defining loadings on Factor-B in the heterogeneous sample.

TABLE 5.12: Tests High on Varimax Factor-BM_{10} in the Homogeneous Sample (together with their Loadings on Heterogeneous Sample Factors)

Sl. No.	SOI	Name of the Test Factor	Loadings	Heterogeneous Sample Factor Loadings		
				A	B	E
33	NMT	Unusual Uses	0.73**		0.61*	0.44
34	NMT	Object Synthesis	0.68**		0.63**	
15	CMT	Social Institutions	0.41**(P)	0.41	0.53*	
27	NMR	Inventive Verbal Relations	0.36		0.50*	

** Defining Test.
* Marker Test.

Out of the three defining tests for Factor-BM_{10}, first two, Unusual Uses Test and Object Synthesis Test emerged with excellent and very good sized loadings respectively; while, third one, i.e., Social Institutions Test emerged with poor sized loading. Therefore, Social Institutions Test was of little consequence to interpret Factor-BM_{10} and only Unusual Uses Test and Object Synthesis Test could be used for its interpretation. Both these tests were presumed to involve the mental operation of convergent production and product category of transformations according to SOI theory. Therefore, Factor-BM_{10} on which these were loaded as defining tests, may be identified as *Convergent Production of Semantic Transformations.*

Factor-CM_6

Table 5.13 shows the tests with significant loadings on Factor-CM_6 in the homogeneous sample together with their loadings on factors in the heterogeneous sample. Out of the three tests which emerged with significant loadings on Factor-CM_6 in the homogeneous sample, only one emerged with defining loading; other two emerged with secondary loadings. Group Classification Test which emerged with defining loading on it, had loadings on three factors in the heterogeneous sample – on Factor-C marker loading, on Factor-A and Factor-G secondary loadings.

As Necessary Arithmetic Operations Test and Word Grouping Test emerged with secondary loadings on Factor-CM_6, therefore, they were of little value for its interpretation. Thus, only Group Classification Test which had an excellent sized loading was useful for interpretation of Factor-CM_6. Group Classification Test was presumed to involve the mental operation of convergent production according to SOI theory. It was presumed to involve the mental operation of convergent production in the heterogeneous samnle also. As it emerged as the only defining test for Factor-CM_6 in the homogeneous sample, it may, therefore, be identified as involving mental operation of 'Convergent Production' in this sample too.

TABLE 5.13: Tests High on Varimax Factor-CM_6 in the Homogeneous Sample (together with their Loadings on Heterogeneous Sample Factors)

Sl. No.	SOI	Name of the Test Factor	Loadings	Heterogeneous Sample Factor Loadings			
				A	B	C	G
24	NMC	Group Classification	0.81**	0.39		0.57*	0.37
10	CMS	Necessary Arithmetic Operations	0.47	0.40	0.42*		
23	NMC	Word Grouping	0.43	0.63*		0.3	

** Defining Test.
* Marker Test.

Further, Group Classification Test was presumed to involve SOI's product category of classes. However, in case of heterogeneous sample it was presumed to involve the product, 'formations'. This would be so in a situation wherein quite a substantial number of subjects were predisposed to arrive at the end results from the given items of information by formations. But ability for semantic formations also subsumes ability to form classes and in case of Factor-CM_6, due to homogeneity of the sample, the product of 'formations' has clearly differentiated into 'classes'. Factor-CM_6 may therefore be identified as *Convergent Production of Semantic Classes.*

Chhikara (1982) also identified a factor; Deduction of Verbal Concepts or Convergent Production of Semantic Classes with Group Classification Test as the leading defining test.

Factor-CM_7

Table 5.14 shows the tests with significant loadings on Factor-CM_7 in the homogeneous sample together with their loadings on the factors in the heterogeneous sample. Out of the five tests which emerged with significant loadings on Factor-CM_7 in the homogeneous sample, two, Gestalt Transformation Test and Temporal Order Test which emerged as defining tests with excellent to very good sized loading on it, were defining tests with good sized loadings on Factor-C in the heterogeneous sample as well; one, Seeing Problems Test which emerges as marker test with good sized loading on it, was marker test with poor sized loadings on Factor-E in the heterogeneous sample but it had same sized secondary loadings on Factor-C and Factor-A in the heterogeneous sample; one, Necessary Facts Test though emerged as defining test yet it had exactly fair sized loading on it; so as discussed earlier, it could be ignored; one, Ship Destination Test emerged as secondary test with poor sized loading on it; so it was of little interpretative value. The last two tests though were of little interpretative value, yet they did indicate the commonness of either operations or of products between Factor-A, Factor-B and Factor-C.

TABLE 5.14: Tests High on Varimax Factor-CM_7 in the Homogeneous Sample (together with their Loadings on Heterogeneous Sample Factors)

Sl. No.	SOI	Name of the Test Factor	Loadings	Heterogeneous Sample Factor Loadings			
				A	B	C	E
32	NMT	Gestalt Transformation	0.72**			0.57**	
30	NMS	Temporal Order	0.65**			0.58**	
18	CMI	Seeing Problems	0.56*	0.37		0.37	0.43*
12	CMS	Necessary Facts	0.45**(P)	0.45*	0.38		
11	CMS	Ship Destination	0.38		0.54**		

** Defining Test.
* Marker Test.

Both Gestalt Transformation Test and Temporal Order Test were presumed to involve the mental operation of convergent production according to SOI theory and in case of heterogeneous sample, too, they emerged as involving mental operation of convergent production. Seeing Problem Test was presumed to involve the mental operation of cognition according to SOI theory, but it divided its loadings on three factors in case of heterogeneous sample, two of which, viz., Factor-A and Factor-B were mixed cognition as well as convergent production factor while one, viz., Factor-C was a convergent production factor. In the homogeneous sample, too, this test divided its loadings on two factors, Factor-EM_3 (mixed cognition as well as convergent production factor) and Factor-CM_7, though with poor sized loading on the former and good sized loading on the later. Considering the fact that both Gestalt Transformation Test and Temporal Order Test were defining variables with excellent to very good sized loadings on Factor-CM_7, and both involved mental operation of convergent production according to SOI theory; also in the heterogeneous sample, it could therefore be presumed that Seeing Problem Test which was poorly loaded on Factor-C (convergent production) in the heterogeneous sample has emerged with good sized marker loading on convergent Production Factor-CM_7. Factor-CM_7 may therefore be identified as involving mental operation of 'Convergent Production'.

Further, Gestalt Transformation Test was presumed to involve SOI's product category of transformations, Temporal Order Test the product category of systems and Seeing Problems Test the product category of implications. However, as all these tests emerged with excellent to good sized loadings on Factor-CM_7, it suggested that they shared a product of information in common, to emerge together. A perusal of the nature of these tests revealed that they all demanded the outcomes or the end results to be produced as 'conformations', from the given items of information. This is so because Gestalt Transformations Test required an examinee to choose an object out of four given objects which could be used in an unusual way. But in this, the object had to conform to the use to which it had to be put. Temporal Order Test required the examinees to produce an order of the given events which would conform to some meaningful sequence. Finally, in each item of Seeing Problems Test an object was given to the examinees and they were asked to write three questions concerning each of those objects which could conform to the usual problems. In heterogeneous sample, the product of information in Gestalt Transformation Test and Temporal Order Test was identified as, 'formations' and in Seeing Problems as, 'connections'. As both these terms, i.e., formations and connections subsume 'conformation' to be either of temporal or of spatial grouping of objects or events, or to their attributes. Hence due to homogeneity of sample these products have differentiated into 'conformations' in case of Factor-CM_7. Factor-CM_7 may therefore be identified as *Convergent Production of Semantic Conformations*.

Factor-DM$_9$

Table 5.15 shows the tests with significant loadings on Factor-DM$_9$ in the homogeneous sample together with their loadings on factors in the heterogeneous sample. Out of the three tests which emerged with significant loadings on Factor-DM$_9$ in the homogeneous sample, one, Logical Classification Test which was its defining test with substantial sized loading, was defining test of Factor-D in the heterogeneous sample as well with very good sized loadings; one, Sentence Classification Test which was its defining test, was defining test of Factor-A in the heterogeneous sample as well but with poor sized loadings on both. Hence, as discussed earlier, it could be ignored. The remaining one, i.e., Word Group Naming Test emerged as secondary test with poor sized loading, so it could also be ignored.

TABLE 5.15: Tests High on Varimax Factor-DM$_9$ in the Homogeneous Sample (together with their Loadings on Heterogeneous Sample Factors)

Sl. No.	SOI Factor	Name of the Test	Loadings	Heterogeneous Sample Factor Loadings	
				A	D
05	CMC	Logical Classification	0.80**		0.68**
06	CMC	Sentence Classification	0.42**(P)	0.37**	
20	NMU	Word Group Naming	0.40	0.61**	

** Defining Test.

Logical Classification Test had the highest and excellent sized defining loading on Factor-DM$_9$. It was presumed to involve the mental operation of cognition and product category of classes according to SOI theory. Therefore, Factor-DM$_9$ may be identified as *Cognition of Semantic Classes.*

Factor-EM$_5$

Table 5.16 shows the tests with significant loadings on Factor-EM$_5$ in the homogeneous sample together with their loading on factors in the heterogeneous sample. Out of the ten tests which emerged with significant loadings on Factor-EM$_5$ in the homogeneous sample five had significant loadings on Factor-A, one on Factor-B and four on Factor-E in the heterogeneous sample.

TABLE 5.16: Tests High on Varimax Factor-EM_5 in the Homogeneous Sample (together with their Loadings on Heterogeneous Sample Factors)

Sl. No.	SOI Factor	Name of the Test	Loading	Heterogeneous Sample Factor Loadings		
				A	B	E
13	CMT	Similarities	0.67**			0.68**
31	NMS	Word Matrix-II	0.60**(T)	0.46**		
14	CMT	Different Meanings	0.56*(T)		0.47**	
22	NMU	Picture Group Naming	0.52**			0.42*
04	CMC	Word Classification	0.52*	0.53**		
20	NMU	Word Group Naming	0.46*(P)	0.61**		
29	NMS	Sentence Order	0.42	0.58**		
26	NMR	Verbal Relations Naming	0.41			0.44*
18	CMI	Seeing Problems	0.39			0.43*
09	CMR	Word Matrix-I	0.38**(P)	0.55**		

** Defining Test.
* Marker Test.
T Test with substantial loading which could be interpreted with differentiated independent factor (DF) on the basis of common elements.
P Test with poor loading which could be ignored.

On the basis of significant loadings Factor-5 of the homogeneous sample could either be named as Factor-AM_5 or Factor-EM_5. However, out of all the ten tests only first one, i.e., Similarities Test emerged with the highest and very good sized defining loading on Factor-5 in the homogeneous sample, and it had highest and very good sized defining loading on Factor-E in the heterogeneous sample as well. The next test i.e., Word Matrix-II emerged with good sized defining loadings on Factor-5 in the homogeneous sample, but it had just fair sized defining loading on Factor-A (a mixed general factor) in the heterogeneous sample. It would well be due to some common elements between Similarities Test and Word Matrix-II Test that the latter has emerged with good sized loading on Factor-5 as compared to just fair sized loading on Factor-A. Similarly, Different Meanings Test which was next to Word Matrix-II Test, emerged with good sized marker loading on Factor-5 in the homogeneous sample but it had just fair sized loading on Factor-B in the homogeneous sample which could again be due to some common elements between Similarities Test and Different Meanings Test. The next test, i.e., Picture Group Naming emerged with fair sized defining loading on Factor-5 in the homogeneous sample and it had poor sizes marker loading on Factor-E in the heterogeneous sample. Next to it, i.e., Word Classification Test emerged with fair sized marker loading on Factor-5 in the homogeneous sample and had almost same sized defining loading on Factor-A in the heterogeneous sample. It would well be due to common elements between Similarities Test, Picture Group Naming Test and Word Classification Test, that the latter had emerged on Factor-5 in the homogeneous sample. Remaining five tests emerged with just fair to poor sized loadings on Factor-5 in the homogeneous sample; therefore they were of little consequence for the purposes of identification. Considering the fact that Factor-A in the heterogeneous sample was a mixed general factor, and sizes of the loadings, Factor-5 may be named Factor-EM_5 and be counted as a differentiated factor of Factor-E of the heterogeneous sample.

According to SOI theory, Similarities, Different Meanings and Word Classification tests were presumed to involve the mental operation of cognition while Word Matrix-II and Picture Group Naming tests were presumed to involve the mental operation of convergent production. This suggested that they all involved a mixed mental operation of cognition as well as convergent production to emerge together on Factor-EM_5. In case of heterogeneous sample, too, these tests had loadings on mixed cognition as well as convergent production factors: Factor-A, Factor-B or Factor-E. Factor-EM_5 may., therefore, be identified as involving mixed mental operation of 'inference'.

Further, Similarities and Different Meanings tests were presumed to involve SOI's product category of transformations, Word Matrix-II Test the product category of systems, Picture Group Naming Test the product category of units and Word Classification Test the product category of classes. However, as all these tests had fair to very good sized loadings on Factor-EM_5, it suggested that they shared the same product of information in common to emerge together on it. A perusal of the nature of these tests revealed that they all required an examinee to infer 'agreements' between or amongst the given items of information in order to arrive at the outcomes or end results. For example, in each item of Similarities Test an examinee had to infer three characteristics or properties between two given objects which should be in agreement with both the objects; in Word Matrix-II Test he had to fill up such words in rows and columns of a (3 × 3) matrix, they should agree with the properties of verbal concepts in a row and in a column; in Different Meanings Test an examinee had to infer four verbal concepts that should agree in meanings to the given verbal concepts; in picture Group Naming Test the examinees had to infer a name that should agree with all the different and diverse elements given either in terms of location, function, utility or common attributes, and in Word Classification Test they had to identify a verbal concept which did not agree with the rest.

Given the semantic information in the test-tasks of the defining and marker tests, Similarities, Word Matrix-II, Different Meaning, Picture Group Naming and Word Classification with the mixed mental operation of cognition as well as convergent production, the products then are those of agreements. Factor-EM_5 can therefore, be identified as *Inference of Semantic Agreements*.

Factor-EM_8

Table 5.17 shows the tests with significant loadings on Factor-EM_8 of the homogeneous sample together with their loadings on Factors of the heterogeneous sample. Out of the two tests which emerged with significant loadings on Factor-EM_8 of homogeneous sample, one, Naming Meaningful Trend Test had good sized marker loading on Factor-E and poor sized loading on Factor-A in the heterogeneous sample while another, i.e., Necessary Arithmetic Operations Test had marker though poor sized loading on Factor-B and almost same sized secondary loading on Factor-A of the heterogeneous sample. The former emerged with very good sized defining loadings on Factor-EM_8, while the latter with only fair sized marker loading. It could well be due to some common elements between Naming Meaningful Trend Test and Necessary Arithmetic Operation Test that the latter has emerged with fair sized loading on Factor-EM_8 as compared to poor sized loading on Factor-B.

Naming Meaningful Trends Test was presumed to involve the mental operation of convergent production according to SOI theory, while Necessary Arithmetic Operations Test was presumed to involve the mental operation of cognition. However, in the present case it may well be that Necessary Arithmetic Operations Test involved mental operation of convergent production as it has emerged with the defining test Naming Meaningful Trend which entailed 'convergent production'. Necessary Arithmetic Operation Test emerged with significant secondary loading on a factor–Factor-CM_6, which was also identified as a convergent production factor. Factor-EM_8 may, therefore, be identified as involving mental operation of 'convergent production'.

TABLE 5.17: Tests High on Varimax Factor-EM_8 of the Homogeneous Sample (together with their Loadings on Heterogeneous Sample Factors)

S. No.	SOI Factor	Name of the Test	Loadings	Heterogeneous Sample Factor Loadings		
				A	B	E
21	NMU	Naming Meaningful Trends	0.69**	0.36		0.55*
10	CMS	Necessary Arithmetic Operations	0.49*	0.40	0.42*	

** : Defining Test.
* : Marker Test.

Further, Naming Meaningful Trend Test was presumed to involve the SOI's product category of units while Necessary Arithmetic Operations Test the product category of systems. However, a perusal of the nature of Necessary Arithmetic Operations Test revealed that it could also be presumed to involve the product category of units. For example, in each of its items an arithmetic problem was given, and an examinee was asked to identify which one of the four fundamental rules: addition, subtraction, multiplication or division or a pair of these, could be used to solve those problems. At the face of it, 'an operation' correctly identified appears to involve the product category of systems, for it is applied to a system delineated by a problem. However, if the same set of operations is repeated, and the problem happens to be a 'rule-of-thumb' type, then the verbal label for an operation may well be reduced to a 'unit'. This is to say, that the operations: addition, subtraction, multiplication or division or a pair of these are amenable to be treated as a 'unit', if the problem happens to be a repeatedly encountered problem which due to its verbal cues does not require special effort to identify the 'system'. For instance, in item No. 3 the problem is: A woman takes two days to knit a sweater; how many days will she take to knit eight sweaters? (1) Add (2) Subtract (3) Multiply (4) Divide, tends to predispose an examinee by 'how many days' verbal cues and everyday use of 'one to many' principle to go straight for the correct response, i.e., the operation tends to become an operation unit which requires little of 'cognition' and more of 'convergent production'. Thus, it can be presumed that the examinees may well have reached the end results by using 'units' of operations on the information contained in the given items.

Given the semantic information in test-tasks of defining and marker tests, Naming Meaningful Trend and Necessary Arithmetic Operations with the mental operation of convergent production the products then are those of units. Factor-EM_8 can, therefore, be identified as *Convergent Production of Semantic Units.*

Factor-FM_3

Table 5.18 shows the tests with significant loadings on Factor-FM_3 in the homogeneous sample together with their loadings on factors in the heterogeneous sample. Out of the four tests which emerged with significant loadings on Factor-3 in the homogeneous sample, one, i.e., Apparatus Test which emerged with excellent sized defining loading on it, had same sized defining loading on Factor-F in the heterogeneous sample as well; one, Missing Links Test which emerged with good sized defining loading on it had only fair sized defining loading on Factor-B in the heterogeneous sample; remaining two, Different Meaning Test and Ship Destination Test emerged with poor sized inconsequential loadings on it, thus they could be ignored. Considering the loadings and the fact that Factor-B was a mixed factor involving both the mental operations of cognition and convergent production, so Missing Links Test has emerged as a defining variable together with a cognition test – Apparatus Test, Factor-3 in the homogeneous sample may be named Factor-FM_3, and Missing Links Test may be considered with Apparatus Test.

TABLE 5.18: Tests High on Varimax Factor-FM_3 in the Homogeneous Sample (together with their Loadings on Heterogeneous Sample Factors)

Sl. No.	SOI Factor	Name of the Test	Loadings	Heterogeneous Sample Factor Loadings	
				B	F
16	CMI	Apparatus Test	0.76**		0.78**
36	NMI	Missing Links	0.59**(T)	0.51**	
14	CMT	Different Meanings	0.40	0.47**	
11	CMS	Ship Destination	0.39*(P)	0.54**	

** Defining Test.
* Marker Test.

Both Apparatus Test and Missing Links Test were presumed to involve SOI's product category of implications. However, the former was presumed to involve the mental operation of cognition while the latter the mental operation of convergent production according to SOI theory. Moreover, as Apparatus Test had much higher loading on Factor-FM_3, it was presumed that Missing Links Test also involved a mental operation common with Apparatus Test. It may be well so as discussed earlier while interpreting Factor-B of the heterogeneous sample that there could be alternative responses which could be accepted as correct, therefore, there was more of 'cognition' than of 'convergent production' (i.e., of arriving at a single correct response) in working out the links. Therefore, Missing Links Test was identified to involve a mixed mental operation of cognition as well as convergent production in the heterogeneous sample (defining variable of Factor-B). So, whatever variance was accounted for by the mixed mental operation of cognition and convergent production in case of heterogeneous sample, was taken over by the mental operation of cognition in case of homogeneous sample. For convergent production does involve cognition and this may well be so in case of Missing Links Test due to which it emerged with Apparatus Test on Factor-FM_3, as also because they both shared the same product of information 'implications'. Factor-FM_3 may, therefore, be identified as *Cognition of Semantic Implications*.

Bala (1977) also identified a similar factor 'Conceptual Foresight or Cognition of Semantic Implications' at the age of 14+ and 15. Tewari, 1985; Singh, 1987; also identified a factor 'Cognition of Semantic Implications' in their studies.

Factor-GM_{11}

Table 5.19 shows significant loadings of only one test, Sequential Association on Factor-GM_{11} of the homogeneous sample together with its loading on Factor-G of the heterogeneous sample. It also shows that Sequential Association Test emerged as defining variable with excellent sized loading on Factor-GM_{11} and had same sized defining loading on Factor-G as well.

Factor-GM_{11} of the homogeneous sample was a signlet factor, determined by Sequential Association Test only. Sequential Association Test was presumed to involve the mental operation of convergent production and product category of implications according to SOI theory. Therefore, Factor-GM_{11} may be identified as *Convergent Production of Semantic Implications.*

TABLE 5.19: Tests High on Varimax Factor-GM_{11} of the Homogeneous Sample (together with their Loadings on Heterogeneous Sample Factors)

Sl. No.	SOI Factor	Name of the Test	Loading	Heterogeneous Sample Factor Loadings G
37	NMI	Sequential Association	0.87**	0.78**

** Defining Test.

Chhikara (1982) also identified a similar factor 'Deduction of Inference or Convergent Production of Semantic Implications'. Tewari (1985) too identified a similar factor 'Convergent Production of Semantic Implication'.

Overview

A number of investigators have been concerned about the problem of relationship between reasoning abilities and achievement in Science and Mathematics (*cf.* Ch. II). On the one hand, as revealed in these investigations, variations in the patterns of reasoning abilities led to the identification of the need to work out sampling criteria for selection of pupils for future investigations. On the other hand, restrictions of these studies to three cognition and convergent production products led to the identification of the need to cover all the six products. Accordingly, the present study was conducted upon two groups of students, one heterogeneous and another homogeneous in terms of 'social context' and 'general intellectual functioning', covering all the six cognition and convergent production products.

I. Factor Results

The scores on thirty-seven reasoning tests were correlated and on factor analyses of the 37 × 37 correlation matrices for heterogeneous and homogeneous samples separately by Principal factor analysis method and rotating according to varimax criterion, seven factors in the heterogeneous sample and eleven factors in the homogeneous sample were identified. These were as given in Table 5.20.

TABLE 5.20: Factor Identified in the Two Samples

SOI Factor	Heterogeneous Sample	Homogeneous Sample
CMU	—	*Factor-AM_1*: Cognition of Semantic Units
CMC	*Factor-D*: Cognition of Semantic Classes	*Factor-DM_9*: Cognition of Semantic Classes
CMR	—	—
CMS	—	—
CMT	—	—
CMI	*Factor-F*: Cognition of Semantic Implications	*Factor-FM_3*: Cognition of Semantic Implications
NMU	—	*Factor-EM_8*: Convergent Production of Semantic Units
NMC	—	*Factor-CM_6*: Convergent Production of Semantic Classes
NMR	—	*Factor-BM_2*: Convergent Production of Semantic Relations
NMS	—	—
NMT	—	*Factor-BM_{10}*: Convergent Production of Semantic Transformations
NMI	*Factor-G*: Convergent Production of Semantic Implications	*Factor-GM_{11}*: Convergent Production of Semantic Implications
Mixed Factors:		
	Factor-A: General Inference of Semantic Products	Factor-AM_4: Inference of Semantic Referents
	Factor-B: Inference of Semantic Mutations	—
	Factor-C: Convergent Production of Semantic Formations	Factor-CM_7: Convergent Production of Semantic Conformations
	Factor-E: Inference of Semantic Connections	Factor-EM_5: Inferring Semantic agreements

It was observed from the above table that out of the twelve SOI's reasoning factors selected for the present investigation, seven were identified in the heterogeneous sample and eleven in the homogeneous sample. Of the seven factors identified in the heterogeneous sample, three, i.e., Factor-D, Factor-F and Factor-G emerged same as SOI factors–CMC, CMI and NMI while four, Factor-A, Factor-B, Factor-C and Factor-E emerged as mixed factors, and of the eleven factors identified in the homogeneous sample eight, Factor-AM_1, Factor-DM_9, Factor-FM_3, Factor-EM_8, Factor-CM_6, Factor-BM_2, Factor-BM_{10} and Factor-GM_{11} emerged same as SOI Factors, CMU, CMC, CMI, NMU,

NMC, NMR, NMT and NMI respectively, while the remaining three emerged as mixed factors.

Thus, these results revealed different patterns of reasoning abilities for the heterogeneous and homogeneous samples, and suggested that the nature of the domain of an investigation very much depended on the nature of the group of individuals studied, more specifically on the homogeneity or heterogeneity of those individuals in terms of social context and general intellectual functioning.

II. Conformity with the Earlier Findings

The SOI factor Cognition of Semantic Implications (CMI) which was identified in both the samples in the present study was identified in three of the studies undertaken earlier in India by Bala (1977), Tewari (1985) and Singh (1987). The SOI Factor Convergent Production of Semantic Implications (NMI) which was also identified in both the samples in the present study, was identified in two of the earlier Indian studies undertaken by Chhikara (1982) and Tewari (1985). However, SOI Factor Cognition of Semantic Classes (CMC) which was also identified in both the samples in the present study, was not identified in any of the earlier Indian studies. Thus the findings of the present study to some extent agree with the findings of the earlier Indian studies. Had earlier Indian investigators factor analyzed all the cognition and convergent production products, there might have been a possibility of getting the conforming results.

III. Differentiation of the Factors

Many Psychologist agree with Garrett (1946), "the abilities that are found by factor analysis come about by differentiation from a single, a general intellectual ability that prevails in infancy and early childhood". Some studies which supported Garrett's assertion found differentiation of abilities by the age of 11 years, some by the age of 13 years or 14 years and some by the age of 15 years or more. Some studies which did not favour Garrett assertion established differentiation of abilities in even very young children down below the age of 3 years (*cf.* Guilford, 1967, pp. 414-415); while others supported increasing clarity of factors with more experience (Mitchell, 1956). However, none of the studies conducted earlier considered that, instead of age, the homogeneity of the sampled individuals in terms of their general intellectual functioning could be the basis for differentiation of abilities (age in the present investigation was controlled by taking both the samples of students of the age of fourteen years). As revealed in the present study, differentiation of reasoning abilities is shown in Table 5.21.

TABLE 5.21: Differentiation of Factors of the Heterogeneous Sample in the Homogeneous Sample

Heterogeneous Sample Factor	Homogeneous Sample Factors
Factor-A	Factor-AM_1 and Factor-AM_4
Factor-B	Factor-BM_2 and Factor-BM_{10}
Factor-C	Factor-CM_6 and Factor-CM_7
Factor-D	Factor-DM_9
Factor-E	Factor EM_5 and Factor-EM_8
Factor-F	Factor-FM_3
Factor-G	Factor-GM_{11}

It can be seen from the above table that almost all the factors except Factor-GM_{11} identified in the homogeneous sample in the present study emerged as differentiated factors of the factors identified in the heterogeneous sample. (Factor GM_{11} was equivalent to Factor-G of the heterogeneous sample.) This suggested that differentiated reasoning abilities the amenable to identification depending upon the homogeneity of the selected individuals in terms of social context and general intellectual functioning.

The significance of this finding lies in the fact that for streaming the pupils to different types of courses, or placement into various types of vocational or professional programmes one of the major criteria should be the homogeneity of the group of pupils in terms of their social context and general intellectual abilities. On the other hand, this also provides empirical evidence for differential education depending upon the homogeneity of the group of pupils for a relevant type of curricular programme in consonance with their pattern (profile) of abilities.

IV. Reasoning as a Concept

Thus the domain of reasoning with which this investigation was concerned may now be conceptualized by seven well defined and empirically established factors stated earlier as Factor-A, Factor-B, Factor-C, Factor-D, Factor-E, Factor-F and Factor-G in case of fourteen year old class IX students of Government Senior Secondary Schools of Delhi, who were heterogeneous in terms of their social context and general intellectual functioning, and by eleven well defined empirically established factors stated earlier as Factor-AM_1, Factor-BM_2, Factor-FM_3, Factor-AM_4, Factor-EM_5, Factor-CM_6, Factor-CM_7, Factor-EM_8, Factor-DM_9, Factor-BM_{10} and Factor-GM_{11} in case of fourteen year old class IX students of Government Senior Secondary Schools of Delhi who were homogeneous in terms of their social context and general intellectual functioning.

6

CONCLUSIONS, SUGGESTIONS AND DELIMITATIONS

THE STUDY was done with the following objectives:

The Objectives

(1) To identify the criteria for grouping of students into a homogeneous and a heterogeneous sample.
(2) To identify the factors that will explain common variance in reasoning ability tests in the homogeneous and heterogeneous samples.
(3) To study the variations in factor patterns of reasoning abilities in the two samples.

The following hypotheses were formulated:

The Hypotheses

(1) Differentiation of reasoning abilities takes place amongst the pupils of 14+ age groups.
(2) It is possible to identify twelve independent SOI reasoning factors, CMU, CMC, CMR, CMS, CMT, CMI, NMU, NMC, NMR, NMS, NMT and NMI as posited by Guilford for the 14+ pupils in the heterogeneous as well as in the homogeneous group.
(3) Different factor patterns of reasoning abilities may be noticed in the heterogeneous and homogeneous groups.

Selection and Construction of Tools

To start with, the investigation required at least three tests for each of the SOI factors, CMU, CMC, CMR, CMS, CMT, CMI, NMU, NMC, NMR, NMS, NMT and NMI. Twenty-seven of such tests, i.e., three tests for each of the factors, CMC, CMR, CMS, CMI, NMC, NMR, NMS and NMI, two tests for the factor, CMT, and one additional test for the factor, CMI were already available. The remaining ten tests, i.e., three for the SOI factor, CMU, one for the SOI factor, CMT, three for the SOI factor, NMU and three for the SOI factor, NMT were developed by the present investigator himself. These were developed according to the sample items given by Guilford and Hoepfner (1971, pp.367-497) and using dichotomous (27 per cent high and low) criterion suggested by Harper, *et al.*, (1962).

Formation of Samples and Collection of Data

For the purpose of collection of data, ten Government Boys' Senior Secondary schools which were considered to be typical of the population of Delhi students were picked up. From each of these schools, one section of class IX was selected to constitute the initial heterogeneous sample of 14+ boys. To obtain the homogeneous sample of students, two criteria were set up. In order to preclude the possibility of the effects due to moderator variables, the first criterion was to pick up the group from schools situated within one officials' colony. In order to preclude the possibility of effects due to uneven maturation of mental ability, the second criterion was to pick up the group from the schools which would be equivalent in terms of means and variances of 'intellectual efficiency' scores. Thus, all such pupils, who belonged to one particular residential colony, were picked up from the heterogeneous sample. Further, Student's '*t*' test for the significance of difference between school means and Fisher's '*F*' test for the equality of two 'within' school variances on Raven's Standard Progressive Matrices Scores were applied to pick up equivalent groups in order to form the homogeneous group. The total number of students in the heterogeneous and homogeneous samples was 325 and 146 respectively.

Analysis of Data and Interpretation of Factors

The correlation co-efficients indicated that the reasoning abilities as measured by the present set of tests, belonged to a 'positive manifold' both in case of the heterogeneous as well as homogeneous sample.

These correlations also indicated that the tests belonging to a particular SOI category were not only viable measures of that category but, at the time provided measures of different facets of that category.

On factor-analyses of the correlation matrices by the principal factor analysis method and rotating according to varimax criterion, seven factors in case of heterogeneous sample and eleven factors in case of homogeneous sample were identified. The seven factors in case of heterogeneous sample were:

Factor-A: General Inference of Semantic Products
Factor-B: Inference of Semantic Mutations
Factor-C: Convergent Production of Semantic Formations
Factor-D: Cognition of Semantic Classes
Factor-E: Inference of Semantic Connections
Factor-F: Cognition of Semantic Implications
Factor-G: Convergent Production of Semantic Implications

The eleven factors in case of homogeneous samples were:

Factor-AM_1: Cognition of Semantic Units
Factor-AM_4: Inference of Semantic Referents
Factor-BM_2: Convergent Production of Semantic Relations
Factor-BM_{10}: Convergent Production of Semantic Transformations
Factor-CM_6: Convergent Production of Semantic Classes
Factor-CM_7: Convergent Production of Semantic Conformations
Factor-DM_9: Cognition of Semantic Classes
Factor-EM_5: Inference of Semantic Agreements
Factor-EM_8: Convergent Production of Semantic Units
Factor-FM_3: Cognition of Semantic Implications
Factor-GM_{11}: Convergent Production of Semantic Implications.

On examination of the factors identified in both the samples in terms of SOI factors, it was found that out of the seven factors identified in case of heterogeneous sample, three were same as SOI factors: CMC, CMI and NMI while four others emerged as mixed factors. Similarly, in case of homogeneous sample out of the eleven factors, eight were same as SOI factors: CMU, CMC, CMI, NMU, NMC, NMR, NMT and NMI while only three emerged as mixed factors. These results supported the hypothesis that different patterns of reasoning abilities may be noticed due to variations in sampling criteria. Again, these result supported the hypothesis that differentiation of reasoning abilities does take place around 14+ and the differentiated dimensions of reasoning abilities are amenable to identification.

The study did not support the hypothesis that it was possible to identify all the twelve independent SOI factors for the 14+ pupils, but it revealed greater number of SOI factors in case of later group, i.e., for the pupils who were similar with regard to their social context and general intellectual efficiency. Perhaps, apart from sex, age, grade and maturation, a more systematic criterion for social context, and some other criterion of 'nurture' may help to identify the factors similar to SOI factors. It was further noticed that out of seven factors, identified in case of the heterogeneous sample, six factors got differentiated in case of the homogeneous sample while one emerged identical in both the samples. This revealed a marked differentiation of reasoning abilities due to similarity of social context and equivalence of maturation of mental ability of subjects.

Suggestions for Further Study

1. Considering the fact that the present study was restricted to content of semantic, studies may be carried out for the content categories of figural, symbolic and behavioural.
2. Considering the fact that the present study has been conducted on boys only, the same may be replicated on similar samples of girls.
3. Considering that greater number of independent SOI reasoning factors were identified in case of homogeneous sample, studies may be carried out by using systematic criteria for 'social context' and for 'nurture' (home background, nutritional status, study patterns etc.) which may well help in identifying clearly differentiated reasoning ability factors in a systematically specified group.
4. Taking note of the finding that pattern of reasoning ability differ for the heterogeneous and homogeneous groups in terms of 'intellectual efficiency' and the 'social context', studies may be carried out on the relationship of reasoning abilities and scholastic achievement in various subjects separately for such heterogeneous and homogeneous groups.

The prospect of such studies is the fact that schools do vary in terms of their intake – some schools having homogeneous groups and some other heterogeneous groups studying in secondary classes. The teachers on the basis of investigations carried out by other investigators on the relationship of reasoning abilities and scholastic aptitude can plan out their curricula and instructional strategies in order to bring their teaching in consonance with the abilities of children.

Delimitations of the Present Study

Keeping in view the limitations of available time and resources, the following delimitations define the scope of the present study:

1. Presuming that the operations of cognition and convergent production adequately subsume reasoning abilities, the present study was limited to the use of tests belonging to these SOI's mental operations (Guilford, 1972).
2. Considering that the interaction in educational institutions is largely in terms of meanings attached to the events, ideas or words, the study was restricted to the content category of 'semantic' of the SOI Model.
3. Considering that by the age of 14+ maturity is achieved in reasoning ability (Guilford, 1967, p.420), and as mental abilities are differentiated from a loosely structured general ability to more clearly separated abilities by this age (Garrett, 1946, p. 373; Dempster, 1948, p. 125), the study was limited to fourteen year old students.
4. Due to limitations of time and resources, the study was limited to Delhi.
5. Delhi is being considered as an inflated official colony and in order to minimize the effects of moderator variables, the study was confined to south zone wherein the largest number of service class people are inhabited.
6. Because of inter-school variations among Government schools, aided schools and public schools, the study was limited to the children studying in Government Senior Secondary Schools only.
7. Because of inter-official colony variations in accommodation patterns (housing) and opportunities for social interaction amongst pupils, the homogeneous sample was delimited to one

colony, viz., Ramakrishna Puram.

8. Because, Government Senior Secondary Schools in South Delhi are Hindi medium schools, the study was limited to those Government Senior Secondary Schools wherein Hindi was the medium of instruction.
9. To avoid the possibility of any sex-generated variance, the study was limited to male students only.

APPENDICES

APPENDIX A

KR-21 Reliability Coefficients

Sl.No.	Name of the test	KR-21 Reliability Coefficients	
		Heterogeneous Sample	Homogeneous Sample
01	Verbal Comprehension	0.829	0.793
02	Word Substitution	0.821	0.804
03	Word Meaning	0.813	0.786
04	Word Classification	0.513	0.490
05	Logical Classification	0.735	0.680
06	Sentence Classification	0.771	0.768
07	Verbal Analogies	0.744	0.689
08	Word Linkage	0.794	0.790
09	Word Matrix - I	0.774	0.744
10	Necessary Arithmetic Operations	0.856	0.835
11	Ship Destination	0.894	0.876
12	Necessary Facts	0.786	0.679
13	Similarities	0.884	0.899
14	Different Meanings	0.701	0.607
15	Social Institutions	0.820	0.811
16	Apparatus Test	0.715	0.731
17	Effect Test	0.925	0.821
18	Seeing Problems	0.672	0.640
19	Pertinent Questions	0.788	0.790
20	Word Group Naming	0.719	0.631
21	Naming Meaningful Trend	0.778	0.727
22	Picture Group Naming	0.592	0.524
23	Word Grouping	0.893	0.871
24	Group Classification	0.933	0.944
25	Figure Concepts	0.549	0.473
26	Verbal Relations Naming	0.848	0.780
27	Inventive Verbal Relations	0.586	0.413
28	Association - IV	0.458	0.463
29	Sentence Order	0.702	0.672
30	Temporal Order	0.959	0.909
31	Word Matrix - II	0.954	0.954
32	Gestalt Transformation	0.581	0.653
33	Unusual Uses	0.716	0.684
34	Object Synthesis	0.591	0.506
35	Syllogisms - III	0.802	0.783
36	Missing Links	0.879	0.851
37	Sequential Association	0.699	0.533

APPENDIX B

* Correlation Matrix for the Heterogeneous Sample# (N=325)

Test	+01	02	03	04	05	06	07	08	09	10	11	12	13	14	15	16	17	18	19	20	21	22	23	24	25	26	27	28	29	30	31	32	33	34	35	36	37
01	—	693	638	537	283	345	446	406	493	462	327	483	275	450	442	145	398	302	468	540	447	372	407	243	366	422	469	304	538	275	449	194	243	355	407	298	107
02		—	622	536	180	385	440	442	519	422	331	458	338	453	506	167	492	405	482	601	505	445	500	298	320	400	523	382	537	335	473	170	332	321	446	318	144
03			—	495	245	330	431	422	465	408	357	464	288	473	494	201	364	290	423	568	409	369	439	290	302	413	393	406	492	293	399	134	327	427	418	339	173
04				—	273	360	343	282	469	417	365	405	345	376	389	197	315	372	437	558	356	436	396	324	266	405	467	319	502	220	501	216	318	332	340	297	086
05					—	276	173	155	279	209	203	218	160	219	221	229	192	099	244	293	237	205	190	144	226	256	188	156	226	057	209	126	068	166	173	196	098
06						—	300	241	415	292	272	294	293	217	252	124	297	224	290	398	273	351	335	254	331	301	357	241	396	224	351	144	232	246	352	243	134
07							—	289	392	323	241	407	221	270	288	087	362	263	313	440	300	307	418	344	354	384	329	249	389	271	426	109	195	275	418	230	080
08								—	308	347	293	361	201	284	269	048	379	305	346	321	279	310	391	286	248	319	315	264	349	149	299	125	268	318	274	192	068
09									—	438	336	451	354	361	419	144	388	363	452	500	431	335	387	241	308	404	463	314	475	246	526	158	311	304	401	333	133
10										—	400	439	328	389	343	065	377	275	375	454	393	350	280	306	290	468	449	325	363	288	443	184	360	355	397	316	144
11											—	410	268	320	428	223	378	258	372	392	358	348	244	212	235	333	406	385	408	316	380	257	345	338	242	342	-025
12												—	320	432	439	108	381	383	418	488	410	429	408	313	340	367	474	386	460	352	446	247	391	376	329	317	104
13													—	383	336	178	369	316	369	368	375	398	191	153	346	316	322	166	286	153	354	147	363	280	188	267	131
14														—	437	118	282	262	362	496	366	460	274	217	345	438	379	272	407	191	318	228	379	349	290	311	059
15															—	149	484	267	447	454	443	407	357	208	294	347	465	365	482	271	421	188	377	402	319	354	080
16																—	166	174	245	157	131	101	092	062	081	121	116	158	144	024	142	102	105	076	128	209	062
17																	—	367	488	457	408	325	390	257	323	407	394	333	468	239	443	146	318	366	392	295	168
18																		—	363	363	362	306	327	200	258	250	314	237	356	327	318	175	222	212	264	201	-013
19																			—	467	336	432	385	244	361	462	447	372	484	244	430	208	348	363	400	263	161
20																				—	511	496	427	297	399	491	505	424	490	305	545	163	331	421	426	350	086
21																					—	445	243	146	429	347	381	229	353	208	374	185	377	281	297	319	072
22																						—	320	216	351	403	488	325	385	332	487	242	365	384	358	334	063
23																							—	633	243	377	461	361	487	297	378	122	191	367	372	242	154
24																								—	216	236	349	202	315	228	319	162	149	230	263	240	173
25																									—	334	319	204	327	221	319	111	345	298	294	204	308
26																										—	443	309	470	248	475	142	335	399	410	299	142
27																											—	481	464	262	446	217	374	432	386	369	147
28																												—	353	329	309	082	229	311	314	284	036
29																													—	294	467	219	274	417	410	328	120
30																														—	304	248	242	218	246	214	193
31																															—	175	350	420	421	308	133
32																																—	222	214	110	226	036
33																																	—	436	158	320	-039
34																																		—	280	325	122
35																																			—	274	139
36																																				—	103
37																																					—

* = Decimal point preceding the entries has been omitted.

\# = 'r' to be significant for d.f.323 at 5 per cent level=0.109 and at 1 per cent level 0.143.

\+ = For test's name please refer to Chapter 3.

APPENDIX C

* Correlation Matrix for the Homogeneous Sample# (N=146)

Test +	01	02	03	04	05	06	07	08	09	10	11	12	13	14	15	16	17	18	19	20	21	22	23	24	25	26	27	28	29	30	31	32	33	34	35	36	37
01	—	634	523	422	260	247	288	407	389	365	158	328	168	359	360	187	296	239	393	386	374	236	315	041	313	325	353	147	463	140	302	179	089	286	334	135	030
02		—	533	437	209	310	318	409	467	212	200	333	233	310	369	270	466	386	417	472	472	317	450	101	225	331	396	239	499	124	385	121	174	263	398	143	109
03			—	489	275	252	257	311	370	189	246	300	244	412	410	280	315	293	409	445	287	234	357	108	160	314	381	381	437	124	259	056	156	337	347	250	134
04				—	305	332	092	281	454	320	307	363	356	336	340	192	275	400	440	509	268	385	279	251	190	375	384	220	455	179	464	257	265	353	267	197	108
05					—	232	037	200	257	182	268	215	122	119	146	241	100	191	233	342	142	177	203	153	163	207	235	069	185	124	160	181	098	179	149	147	038
06						—	195	220	374	176	163	124	272	143	194	129	323	199	314	272	193	257	258	135	279	261	292	035	409	042	322	107	167	217	259	087	162
07							—	270	223	193	185	174	171	118	080	047	300	126	225	159	120	043	307	198	314	204	105	022	240	076	218	-001	084	090	267	108	038
08								—	301	320	301	253	197	186	243	061	389	317	406	303	252	268	392	200	224	294	283	214	332	081	293	146	186	280	247	176	035
09									—	343	287	312	334	252	359	111	368	356	420	410	359	269	392	125	257	430	372	310	379	208	461	113	228	236	352	242	075
10										—	358	390	188	289	242	159	235	231	252	237	304	241	201	333	183	322	314	194	216	263	304	134	231	193	296	175	139
11											—	480	320	287	371	318	383	328	306	257	192	282	247	216	237	192	355	277	329	276	298	351	358	247	189	322	-061
12												—	277	392	352	191	334	468	377	318	204	378	337	148	230	286	402	202	307	280	328	292	318	344	241	283	046
13													—	370	275	235	307	241	341	277	239	348	149	117	234	188	126	069	267	068	360	148	253	187	133	218	206
14														—	396	279	157	327	331	273	213	406	186	090	254	311	229	168	423	062	293	230	256	291	197	192	-062
15															—	206	371	242	413	290	217	248	237	-004	181	268	349	352	348	182	337	195	285	364	286	286	063
16																—	177	198	306	178	110	102	160	115	092	207	176	189	150	134	093	208	130	149	209	337	076
17																	—	290	501	381	267	246	365	178	307	398	349	275	402	228	346	144	193	262	423	200	189
18																		—	415	355	342	313	360	118	207	286	276	198	423	280	262	258	117	231	194	235	017
19																			—	363	159	364	347	130	312	432	363	322	445	251	365	242	340	318	388	125	095
20																				—	359	331	367	147	321	380	240	231	337	148	438	-001	088	232	325	116	021
21																					—	408	202	068	383	226	168	035	231	148	272	077	225	220	269	173	119
22																						—	216	101	276	262	311	146	356	233	414	175	300	334	227	242	092
23																							—	326	138	389	453	311	381	166	333	097	174	322	308	170	123
24																								—	087	118	210	067	067	102	243	166	111	053	116	205	134
25																									—	237	102	078	349	170	257	046	248	229	299	119	004
26																										—	300	314	448	206	415	061	149	146	382	167	128
27																											—	471	333	057	294	215	201	308	276	272	081
28																												—	243	260	131	-037	074	242	176	188	-026
29																													—	170	388	150	169	294	396	230	117
30																														—	168	284	161	108	169	158	126
31																															—	107	267	347	269	148	103
32																																—	188	141	008	240	011
33																																	—	386	165	136	-033
34																																		—	192	240	028
35																																			—	133	151
36																																				—	019
37																																					—

* = decimal point preceding the entries has been omitted.
\# = 'r' to be significant at 5 per cent level=0.163 and at 1 per cent level=0.214.
\+ = For test's name please refer to Chapter 3.

APPENDIX D

Results of the Factor Analyses

TABLE I: Eigen values in case of Heterogeneous Sample

Factor	Eigen value	PCT of VAR	CUM PCT
1	12.91410	34.9	34.9
2	1.61036	4.4	39.3
3	1.31515	3.6	42.8
4	1.21127	3.3	46.1
5	1.12900	3.1	49.1
6	1.07368	2.9	52.0
7	1.01521	2.7	54.8
8	0.96901	2.6	57.4
9	0.95817	2.6	60.0
10	0.85707	2.3	62.3
11	0.83661	2.3	64.6
12	0.79924	2.2	66.7
13	0.79194	2.1	68.9
14	0.76820	2.1	70.9
15	0.72784	2.0	72.9
16	0.70480	1.9	74.6
17	0.65584	1.8	76.6
18	0.63939	1.7	78.3
19	0.62905	1.7	80.0
20	0.59492	1.6	81.6
21	0.56247	1.5	83.1
22	0.54404	1.5	84.6
23	0.53970	1.5	86.1
24	0.52144	1.4	87.5
25	0.47192	1.3	88.8
26	0.46630	1.3	90.0
27	0.44503	1.2	91.2
28	0.42103	1.1	92.4
29	0.41530	1.1	93.5
30	0.38701	1.0	94.5
31	0.36775	1.0	95.5
32	0.32838	0.9	96.4
33	0.32252	0.9	97.3
34	0.29474	0.8	98.1
35	0.26515	0.7	98.8
36	0.23320	0.6	99.4
37	0.21411	0.6	100.0

TABLE II: Principal Factors and Communality Estimates in Case of Heterogeneous Sample

Test*	Factors							Commu-nality
	1	2	3	4	5	6	7	
01	-.71860	-.13354	-.18405	-.15348	-.19737	.09675	-.19494	.67796
02	-.75925	-.13925	-.08598	-.15233	-.22372	.01274	.02204	.67729
03	-.71660	-.12986	-.09019	-.03516	-.18026	.25467	-.09987	.64707
04	-.67540	-.03589	-.12354	.05512	-.10325	-.05432	-.18308	.52289
05	-.35803	.00392	-.47637	.30947	.06823	-.03599	-.34826	.57813
06	-.52848	-.10998	-.18612	.04348	.17766	-.21367	-.16564	.43257
07	-.57113	-.30285	-.02226	-.19180	.01097	-.15085	-.09173	.48648
08	-.52283	-.15203	.11202	-.15679	-.07125	.07835	.07699	.35074
09	-.67782	-.05162	.18620	-.04828	-.03254	-.07100	-.00973	.50530
10	-.63424	.03970	-.05513	-.06174	.14742	.11188	-.04260	.44675
11	-.57276	.26234	.18573	.26333	.18492	.04585	-.00663	.53706
12	-.68371	.04293	.17619	-.02759	-.03869	-.05022	-.06654	.50955
13	-.51517	.33850	-.18363	-.07351	.27091	-.19168	.25131	.59240
14	-.60993	.23218	-.05355	-.11152	.06818	.15502	-.23069	.52312
15	-.65645	.16935	.02827	.03955	-.12628	.21031	.11093	.53445
16	-.24013	.14696	-.38848	.57127	-.26492	.14133	.19372	.68421
17	-.63856	-.01656	-.03091	-.01238	.00235	-.02469	.45016	.61240
18	-.51132	.04247	.08525	-.08245	-.26745	-.50129	.24868	.66197
19	-.67097	.03459	-.09775	.08160	-.03684	-.00467	.26324	.53830
20	-.76176	.00120	-.11145	-.10524	-.06909	.03252	-.10171	.51995
21	-.61427	.27526	-.16433	-.21945	-.02302	-.11470	.01813	.54227
22	-.64411	.21530	.08130	-.06727	.12546	-.06551	-.08600	.49979
23	-.61566	-.49782	.20479	.09104	.02356	-.06850	.00972	.67995
24	-.45495	-.46985	.27011	.19656	.25058	-.17186	-.10700	.64310
25	-.52408	.14801	-.12553	-.29544	.21346	-.21891	-.03858	.49409
26	-.64521	-.01073	-.07155	-.05760	.18791	.16175	.01337	.48469
27	-.70503	-.02284	.13872	.07422	.01828	.17341	-.00220	.55275
28	-.53682	-.05303	.21573	.18581	-.30874	.24579	.10749	.53934
29	-.70820	-.13017	.00217	.04390	-.09021	.02417	-.08772	.52921
30	-.44738	-.03321	.43848	.07775	-.05989	-.28999	.00646	.48728
31	-.68099	-.02772	-.00543	-.03569	.11818	-.05552	.05266	.49674
32	-.30936	.25669	.27841	.35297	.12597	-.28672	-.31532	.56120
33	-.52211	.46294	.23421	-.09789	.16542	.08448	.05559	.58894
34	-.58155	.11688	.21170	.04327	.22180	.30952	.03370	.54468
35	.58111	-.26486	-.10137	-.05973	.00229	.00614	.05724	.42500
36	.50657	.18493	.05245	.32675	.09184	.11577	-.06054	.42583
37	-.17997	-.31285	-.18969	.26210	.52200	.13351	.32795	.63280

* For test's name please refer to Chapter 3.

TABLE III: Varimax Rotated Factors in Case of Heterogeneous Sample

Test*	Factors						
	1	2	3	4	5	6	7
01	.72912	.22957	-.01117	.22812	.17340	.04247	-.09801
02	.73601	.22619	.06682	.02188	.23917	.14296	-.04283
03	.68447	.38123	-.02891	.14864	.05537	.08509	.00058
04	.53402	.24529	.16993	.28691	.20387	.15144	-.04292
05	.21996	.06787	-.00705	.67863	.09303	.22049	.08617
06	.37415	.04555	.22794	.34578	.30480	.03664	.15728
07	.60866	-.00098	.22075	.07776	.21847	-.08743	.07651
08	.50500	.22559	.09710	-.12679	.12725	-.02538	.04984
09	.54661	.18591	.08398	.17382	.32726	.15387	.06248
10	.39929	.41634	.11658	.09730	.26921	-.06329	.12016
11	.22835	.54399	.25289	.05149	.10566	.30829	-.12715
12	.45364	.38340	.29834	.03476	.25066	.03782	-.04780
13	.10259	.24277	.03175	.04822	.67707	.17635	.17343
14	.34722	.46932	-.00125	.26396	.31095	-.08362	-.09458
15	.41025	.53072	-.00110	-.01624	.19901	.21107	-.00757
16	.04307	.06480	.00590	.25520	.03747	.77992	.06548
17	.43634	.26691	.06185	-.22631	.36767	.30320	.26192
18	.37354	-.03588	.37326	-.22117	.42793	.35131	-.16235
19	.43949	.31673	.07175	-.02418	.31750	.32733	.17647
20	.61029	.32575	.07372	.18395	.31011	.07156	-.02860
21	.36139	.25803	-.00379	.09832	.55465	.10592	-.12864
22	.30222	.41117	.22069	.12742	.41680	-.01539	-.02199
23	.63318	.11690	.42639	-.02442	-.04533	.00510	.28444
24	.39106	.06385	.56922	.09589	-.05596	-.11069	.37082
25	.29854	.11301	.09462	.12614	.59667	-.10566	.01203
26	.43802	.38349	.01326	.13062	.28294	-.03090	.22206
27	.47973	.50394	.18072	.04639	.12521	.05880	.12127
28	.44412	.46825	.12828	-.13391	.14227	.25972	-.02733
29	.58781	.30110	.18535	.08762	.15249	.14773	.07690
30	.24469	.20673	.58018	-.15332	.13050	.05875	-.06374
31	.46303	.29280	.19280	.07254	.35078	.06071	.16556
32	.-10662	.30958	.57446	.30111	.12889	.07437	-.10571
33	.06437	.60688	.12061	-.06451	.43809	-.04791	-.05974
34	.26096	.62721	.09456	.00233	.15345	-.08855	.20700
35	.57800	.10937	.08579	.05406	.16270	.06461	.19500
36	.14271	.50709	.18509	.22714	.10008	.19656	.11755
37	.07051	.04399	-.02740	.06805	.04861	.06520	.78351

* For test's name please refer to Chapter 3.

TABLE IV: Eigen Values in Case of Homogeneous Sample

Factor	Eigen value	PCT of VAR	CUM PCT
1	10.33908	27.9	27.9
2	2.01077	5.4	33.4
3	1.61327	4.4	37.7
4	1.52230	4.1	41.9
5	1.30176	3.5	45.4
6	1.24838	3.4	48.7
7	1.23221	3.3	52.1
8	1.18835	3.2	55.3
9	1.06746	2.9	58.2
10	1.03474	2.8	61.0
11	1.00738	2.7	63.7
12	0.96329	2.6	66.3
13	0.86088	2.3	68.6
14	0.84911	2.3	70.9
15	0.78379	2.1	73.0
16	0.74860	2.0	75.1
17	0.73038	2.0	77.0
18	0.70404	1.9	78.9
19	0.68402	1.8	80.8
20	0.62549	1.7	82.5
21	0.59659	1.6	84.1
22	0.58458	1.6	85.7
23	0.57194	1.5	87.3
24	0.51982	1.4	88.6
25	0.48615	1.3	89.9
26	0.47083	1.3	91.2
27	0.44151	1.2	92.4
28	0.41478	1.1	93.5
29	0.38180	1.0	94.6
30	0.33933	0.9	95.5
31	0.31248	0.8	96.3
32	0.30050	0.8	97.1
33	0.26973	0.7	97.9
34	0.22925	0.6	98.5
35	0.19870	0.5	99.0
36	0.19135	0.5	99.5
37	0.17508	0.5	100.0

TABLE V: Principal Factors and Communality Estimates in Case of Homogeneous Sample

Test*	Factors											Communality
	1	2	3	4	5	6	7	8	9	10	11	
01	-.62268	-.27797	.02430	.22599	-.11815	.30859	-.18220	-.01300	-.10556	.21316	-.07536	.72148
02	-.69032	-.33361	.06247	.16254	-.10290	.16929	-.04846	-.00511	-.05683	.23972	.00401	.72049
03	-.63649	-.17533	.25534	.28205	-.16389	.09016	.07669	-.11143	-.16316	.01335	-.00413	.66072
04	-.67645	.02090	.02091	.07750	-.32050	-.24208	.10319	.03762	.08272	-.01583	.05304	.64776
05	-.38247	.07226	.05163	-.02642	-.48135	.09105	-.15639	.01530	.18611	-.29692	-.45230	.74692
06	-.46904	-.23172	-.20197	-.10809	-.17684	-.19099	.16404	-.21732	.29002	-.01263	-.22348	.60110
07	-.35342	-.31938	-.08393	-.32191	.25073	.38751	-.03946	-.33606	.02352	-.01213	.17196	.69537
08	-.54590	-.13265	.05018	-.13563	.10926	.08232	-.28247	-.14483	.06755	.18806	.01199	.49613
09	-.65348	-.15466	.00770	-.03446	-.01117	-.14772	-.03077	.11732	.01004	-.12899	-.02258	.50611
10	-.50609	.12397	-.04409	-.32442	.02566	.04474	-.19000	.12704	-.39417	-.07848	-.00254	.59513
11	-.55485	.47317	.02699	-.14842	.13995	.13019	-.02773	-.09122	.07662	-.18144	-.03799	.64036
12	-.60935	.34078	-.00223	-.01951	.09620	.05298	-.14925	.09756	.01500	.09229	.13712	.55922
13	-.47533	.13753	.37722	.01404	-.10876	-.14663	.34739	-.17109	-.02876	-.11357	-.27343	.65907
14	-.53665	.20994	-.15367	.37665	-.02600	.09159	.01655	-.11000	-.10485	-.07925	.38398	.68370
15	-.57824	.15535	.13472	.29283	.18943	-.07331	.18541	-.05159	-.11188	.05876	-.07420	.56216
16	-.36528	.27243	.17161	.05770	-.27060	.34118	.41282	-.14468	-.07924	-.21608	-.08438	.68390
17	-.61976	-.14753	.05237	-.21759	.27078	.02696	.24912	-.02116	.12474	.08532	-.04152	.61708
18	-.56975	.13632	-.00009	.03256	-.09435	.12598	-.11826	.30247	.22930	.12189	.28117	.62097

Contd.

TABLE V *Contd.*

Test*	Factors											Commu-nality
	1	2	3	4	5	6	7	8	9	10	11	
19	-.58510	.00094	.04590	.03068	.13728	-.03036	.18696	.00043	.31788	.02853	-.02394	.62597
20	-.58277	-.21032	.10464	-.09416	.07137	-.10417	.09839	.21460	.08559	-.21526	.16054	.55479
21	-.58450	.08039	.40668	-.02577	-.01995	-.21751	-.12472	-.14129	-.06690	.13741	-.10269	.63128
22	-.41463	.05682	.62008	.10376	.28177	-.18385	.06131	.15360	-.10124	-.20108	-.00047	.76135
23	-.61333	-.24785	-.04784	.10113	-.19010	-.04748	-.13817	.18510	.03901	-.33595	.01397	.65644
24	-.48818	-.14411	-.38279	.08266	-.05513	.13731	-.14101	.25716	-.38953	.10404	-.15656	.70743
25	-.55343	.17016	-.33555	.12535	-.00616	-.23504	-.05448	-.16539	-.09682	.06792	.05095	.56573
26	-.58828	-.16980	.30365	-.22776	-.00895	-.12738	-.18525	-.09576	.07884	.11004	.09053	.60530
27	-.28326	.11746	.05272	-.63929	-.23230	-.06120	-.19559	-.22998	-.15832	-.11111	.14351	.71237
28	-.44990	-.13413	-.43229	-.01551	.27518	.24916	-.01006	.00137	.05685	-.23705	-.19236	.64185
29	-.66865	-.15809	-.01057	.13762	.00739	.05994	.14548	-.02600	.21593	.07551	.14462	.58988
30	-.33637	.27290	.04241	-.25793	.16802	.13919	.11941	.60274	.07917	.05367	-.14179	.71035
31	-.61007	-.07232	-.23465	-.09164	.00940	.34715	-.07863	-.01654	.01982	-.11111	.14555	.60185
32	-.30131	.54242	-.05181	-.10924	-.20800	.21414	-.01765	.01482	.31034	.38129	-.03812	.73242
33	-.40426	.34275	-.28500	.02734	.32347	-.20361	-.06037	.21731	-.02642	.01776	-.28102	.63983
34	-.50758	.16550	-.02530	.23031	.15739	-.24421	-.13049	-.23133	-.08745	.16625	-.26825	.60091
35	-.53220	-.30114	.03206	-.11070	.17845	.14952	.20740	.03367	-.09885	-.06782	-.16471	.52705
36	-.38472	.37893	.13356	-.05213	-.09063	.17552	.13499	-.16273	-.27506	-.06820	.03974	.47777
37	-.15321	-.16745	-.06790	-.35318	-.25083	-.22221	.53218	.12696	-.26811	.36479	-.07073	.80244

* For test's name please refer to Ch. 3.

TABLE VI: Varimax Rotated Factors in Case of Homogeneous Sample

Test*	Factors										
	1	2	3	4	5	6	7	8	9	10	11
01	.75726	.01414	.10444	.19094	.08811	-.00119	.08347	.25117	.12560	.07288	-.03952
02	.74409	.11557	.06934	.23211	.20553	.01874	.08472	.15103	.08749	.05923	.10497
03	.61924	.28037	.35594	.07580	.20697	-.00422	-.07586	.05808	.13479	.08511	.05133
04	.36963	.15927	.05878	-.06855	.52387	.18020	.16575	.04768	.32895	.16743	.06853
05	.15324	.02222	.19257	-.00179	.03316	.11484	.11893	.08466	.80127	.05882	-.06888
06	.20099	-.06822	-.05690	.33670	.32001	.05660	-.01749	-.17228	.41577	.22291	.28509
07	.27903	-.09615	.06628	.67186	.01558	.33580	-.04661	-.01724	-.15604	-.06146	-.09412
08	.46149	.07878	-.09099	.28388	.08370	.31588	.17162	.02870	.02438	.21098	-.07688
09	.27646	.32631	-.00685	.22335	.37974	.13662	.07528	.17608	.23249	.12358	.06689
10	.10383	.17846	.15490	.11413	.12330	.46601	.14385	.49221	.01559	.13421	.04334
11	-.03371	.17754	.38617	.23023	.16842	.25971	.38270	.05125	.11669	.32825	-.19812
12	.22029	.17188	.18423	.05866	.27953	.21000	.44790	.17536	-.06185	.26504	-.12682
13	-.01482	-.10696	.32570	.18242	.66795	.05988	.02048	.00037	-.03407	.15479	.18099
14	.30125	.00670	.39348	.00588	.55569	-.03595	.09409	.10094	-.16490	.14369	-.24713
15	.28955	.34661	.31060	.09674	.21602	-.13990	.10043	.05527	-.05125	.41005	.04697
16	.09981	.08041	.76080	.10764	.05959	-.03522	.10378	-.03481	.23069	-.03085	.07824
17	.22881	.29470	.06315	.55004	.17555	.09587	.20766	-.02688	-.00247	.17857	.23577
18	.33184	.13220	.03747	.05194	.38801	.06823	.55550	.08698	.03529	-.07446	-.10548

(Contd.)

TABLE VI (*Contd.*)

Test*	Factors										
	1	2	3	4	5	6	7	8	9	10	11
19	.27106	28358	.10236	.38549	.34054	-.04815	.31215	.13428	.14950	.23528	.07153
20	.31231	26112	.00634	.16625	.46021	.06599	-.01584	.25745	.40301	-.07159	-.11319
21	.34859	09642	.01452	.12537	.19951	-.01034	.05550	.69107	.07684	.14655	.11276
22	.14090	03759	.00745	-.01937	.52283	.01470	.21514	.31853	.02969	.34233	.06814
23	.43935	34036	-.08196	.16964	.15989	.42847	.12959	-.11059	.09327	.10092	.06285
24	-.02997	-01341	.12591	.06435	.10365	.80931	.04636	.02321	.11590	-.01733	.09560
25	.05122	-07729	.03854	.61084	.20448	-.07995	.04191	.34273	.16702	.19692	-.15665
26	.18038	45150	-.00431	.30628	.41067	.10195	.10393	.09108	.11828	-.09425	.05883
27	.41069	42140	.11452	-.05376	.06708	.30793	.10873	-.08718	.12302	.35772	.08470
28	.13984	83026	.16534	.00657	.02211	.03645	.03516	-.01829	-.02235	.12664	-.07062
29	.45300	15734	.11240	.33169	.41977	-.06066	.19630	-.08115	.06617	.07211	.04977
30	-.12556	32178	.03567	.16920	-.02158	-.03423	.64563	.33646	.07359	-.01166	.15376
31	.13502	.15046	-.10294	.18005	.60347	.25377	.02572	.12051	.11068	.24096	.06016
32	.12749	-.24025	.22668	-.07407	.02234	.10591	.71847	-.13905	.10689	.20219	.04476
33	-.08055	-.00155	.07464	.18558	.16868	.05872	.11203	.12023	.03588	.72823	-.05292
34	.29439	.13087	.06257	.00408	.14093	.02280	.02256	.05472	.07224	.68117	-.00918
35	.27082	27090	.12536	.51552	.06781	.01458	-.02225	.20678	.09781	.06021	.19172
36	.09054	.09992	.58743	-.00519	.06760	.23640	.13160	.09867	-.02633	.16128	.01642
37	.04548	-.00138	.06015	.02439	.08896	.09459	.01706	.09384	-.04179	-.05388	.87495

* For test's name please refer to Ch. 3.

APPENDIX E

Advice of Prof. Guilford

P.O. Box 1288
Beverly Hills, California
90213

January 6, 1982

Mr. K.P. Garg
Sri Aurobindo Marg
New Delhi 110016

Dear Mr. Garg

I am interested to know that you are planning for research with a factor analysis of reasoning tests at an adolescent level.

I have gone over your list of tests that you are considering in comparison with my list of recommended tests. They are recommended by virtue of having the highest loadings on their salient factors and being most nearly unique measures of their factors.

I am sorry that I do not have a supply of the tests from which I could send sample copies. The tests were turned over to a publisher, who I regret to say does not ordinarily sell tests in India, frankly because it has experienced difficulty in collecting for sales there.

I can suggest that in your own country there have been efforts to develop tests for numerous structure-of-intellect factors and presumably makes them available. The person in charge is Dr. Usha Khire, of the Institute of Intellect and Mind, Jnana Prabodhini, 510, Sadashiv Peth, Pune 411030. I hope she can do something for you.

Sincerely,

(sd/-)
J.P. Guilford
Enc. Marked list of tests

Marked List of Tests

Name of the factor		Name of the test
CMU		Guilford-Zimmerman (39)
	—	Verbal comprehension
	—	Word completion (39)
		Reading comprehension (USAF)
		Verbal opposites (C.G.)
	—	Word substitution
		Sentence synthesis
		Story Titles
		Transitions (Coherence)
CMS		Problem solving (39)
	—	Ship destination
	—	Necessary Facts (31)
		CAT Arithmetic Reasoning
	—	Arithmetic Reasoning (A.A.F.)
		Essential Operations
		Necessary Arithmetic Operations (14)
		Word Matrices
		Circle-Square-Triangle
		Guilford-Zimmerman General Reasoning
CMT		Cartoons (II)
		Social Institutions (II)
	—	Similarities (32)
	—	Seeing Different Meanings
	—	Definitions
		Implied Uses
		Seeing Puzzle Meanings
NMU	—	Word-Group naming (39)
	—	Naming Meaningful Trends (39)
	—	Picture-Group Naming (39)
		Paired Similarities
		Naming Trends
		Verbal Relations Naming
NMS	—	Sentence order (34)
		Picture Arrangement (34)
	—	Temporal Ordering (10)
	—	Ordering I
		Outlining
NMT	—	New uses
	—	Gestalt Transformations (22)
	—	Object Synthesis (11)
		Picture Gestalt (32)
		Predicaments

NB: Figure in brackets indicate the number of the reports from the Psychological laboratory where the test has been described as has been mentioned in your books. Sources of the other tests are not known.

BIBLIOGRAPHY

Books

Anastasi, A., *Individual Differences.* New York: John Wiley, 1965.

Anstey, E., Psychological Tests. London: Nelson, 1966.

Binet A., and Simon Th., *New Methods for the Diagnosis of the Intellectual Level of Subnormals*, Annee Psychol., 1905, 11, pp. 191-244. Reproduced from A. Anastasi, Individual Differences. New York: John Wiley, 1965.

Boring, E.G., *A History of Experimental Psychology* (2nd Ed.). New York: Appelton-century, Grofts, 1950.

Brown, W. and Thomson, G.H., *The Essentials of Mental Measurements.* Cambridge London: Cambridge University Press, 1921.

Bruner, J.S., Goodnow, J.J. and Austin., *A Study of Thinking.* New York: John Wiley, 1956.

Bruner, J.S., *The Process of Education.* Cambridge London: Harward University Press, 1963.

Bruner, J.S., *The Relevance of Education.* London: George Allen, 1972.

Carroll, J.B., "The Measurement of Intelligence" in R.J. Sternberg's *Handbook of Human Intelligence.* Cambridge London: Cambridge University Press, 1982, pp. 29-109.

Cattell, R.B., *Factor Analysis.* New York: Harper, 1952.

Cattell, J. Mck., *Mental Tests and Measurements*, Mind, 1890, 15, pp. 373-381. Reproduced from A. Anastasi, Individual Differences. New York: John Wiley, 1965, pp.25-26.

Comrey, A.L., *A First Course in Factor Analysis.* New York: Academic Press, 1973.

Dashiell, J.F., *Fundamentals of General Psychology* (3rd Ed.). Boston: Houghton Mifflin, 1949, pp. 556-558.

Dempster, J.J.B., *Selection for Secondary Schools.* London: Methuen, 1954.

Deway, John, *Psychology.* London: Harper, 1899, pp. 90-204.

Du Bois, P.H., *A History of Psychological Testing*. Boston: Allgn & Bacon, 1970.

Ebel, R.L., *Measuring Educational Achievement*. New Jersey: Englewood Cliffs, 1965.

Edwards, R., *The Secondary Technical School*. London: University of London Press, 1960.

Ellis, R.S., *Educational Psychology: A Problem Approach*. New York: D. Van Nostrand, 1965, pp. 219-220.

Eston, J.A., Joseph, T. and Frederic, B.K., *Introduction to General Psychology*, D.C. Health, 1953, pp. 363-364.

Eysenck, H.J., *The Structure and Measurement of Intelligence*. New York: Springer-Verlog, 1979.

Eysenck, H.J., Versus Kamin L., *Intelligence: The Battle for the Mind*. London: Pan Book, 1981.

Ferguson, George A., *Statistical Analysis in Psychology and Education*. New York: McGraw-Hill, 1966.

Galton, F., *Inquiries into Human Faculty and Its Development*. Reproduced from A. Anastasi, Individual Differences. New York: John Wiley, 1965, pp. 13-20.

Garrett, H.E. *General Psychology*, New York: American Book Company, 1955, p. 414.

Garrett, H.E., *Elementary Statistics*. New York: Longman, 1956.

Ghorpada, M.B., *Essential of Psychology*. Bombay: Himalaya Publishing House, 1977.

Guilford, J.P., *Psychological Methods*. New York: McGraw-Hill, 1954.

Guilford, J.P., *General Psychology*. Princeton: D. Van Nostrand, 1964, pp. 440-453.

Guilford, J.P., *The Nature of Intelligence*. New York: McGraw-Hill, 1967.

Guilford, J.P., and Hoepfner, R., *The Analysis of Intelligence*. New York: McGraw-Hill, 1971.

Guilford, J.P., *Way Beyond the IQ – Guide to Improving Intelligence and Creativity*. New York: Creative Education Foundation, 1977.

Harman, H.H., *Modern Factor Analysis*. Chicago: University of Chicago Press, 1976.

Kelley, T.L., *Interpretation of Educational Measurements*. New York: World Book Company, 1927.

Kelley, T.L., *Crossroads in the Mind of Man: A Study of Differentiable Mental Abilities*. Standard Cali: Standard University Press, 1928.

Kundu, C.L., *Mental Abilities and School Curriculum*. New Delhi: Vishal, 1978.

Meeker, M.N., *The Structure of Intellect – Its Interpretation and Uses*. Columbus Ohir: Charles E. Merrill, 1969.

Norman, L.M., *The Fundamental of Human Adjustment* (2nd Ed.). Boston: Honghton Mifflin, 1951.

Russell, D.H., *Children's Thinking*. Boston: Ginn, 1956.

Spearman, C., *Abilities of Man*. New York: Macmillan, 1927.

Stanley, J.C., *Measurement in To-day's Schools*. New Jersey: Englewood Cliffs, 1984.

Sternberg, R.J., Reasoning, Problem Solving, and Intelligence. By the same author in *Handbook of Human Intelligence*. Cambridge London: Cambridge University Press, 1982.

Sternberg, R.J., *Beyond IQ*. Cambridge London: Cambridge University Press, 1985.

Thomson, G.H., *The Factorial Analysis of Human Abilities*. London: University of London Press, 1939.

Thorndike, E.L., *et al., The Measurement of Intelligence*. New York: Teachers College, 1927.

Throndike, R.L., *Personnel Selection*. New York: John Wiley, 1949.

Thurstone, L.L., *Primary Mental Abilities*. Chicago: University of Chicago Press (1938), 1957.

Vernon, P.E., *The Measurement of Abilities*. London: University of London Press, 1940.

Vernon, P.E., and Parry, J.B., *Personnel Selection in the British Forces*. London: University of London Press, 1949.

Vernon, P.E., *The Structure of Human Abilities*. London: Methuen, 1950 (1971).

Vernon, P.E., *The Measurement of Abilities* (II Ed.). London: University of London Press Ltd., 1956.

Journals and Periodicals

Alexander, W.P., Intelligence Concrete and Abstract. Brit. *J. Psychol. Monogr. Suppl.*, 1935, 19.

Anastasi, A., The Influence of Specific Experience Upon Mental Organization. *Genet. Psychol. Monogr.*, 1936, 18, pp. 245-355.

Berger, R.M., Guilford, J.P., and Christensen, P.R., A Factor – Analytic Study of Planning. *Psychol. Mongr.*, 1957, 71, No.6.

Blakey, R., A Re-analysis of a Test of the Theory of Two Factors. *Psychometrika*, 1940, 5, pp. 121-136.

Blakey, R.I., A Factor Analysis of a Non-Verbal Reasoning Test. *Educ. Psychol. Measmt.*, 1941, 1, pp. 187-198.

Burt, C., Experimental Test of General Intelligence. *Brit. J. Psychol.*, 1909, 3, pp. 94-177.

Burt, C., The Development of Reasoning in School Children. *J. Exp. Pedag.*, 1919, 5, 36, pp. 8-71.

Burt, C., The Structure of the mind: A Review of the Results of Factor Analysis. *Brit. J. Educ. Psychol.*, 1949, 19, pp. 100-111 and 176-199.

Burt, C., The Evidence for the Concept of Intelligence. *Brit. J. Educ. Psychol.*, 1955, 25, pp. 150-177.

Botzum, W.A., A Factorial Study of Reasoning and Closure Factors. *Psychometrika*, 1951, 16, No. 4, pp. 361-381.

Carroll, J.B., A Model of School Learning. *Teachers College Record*, 1963, 64, pp. 723-733.

Cliff, N., Orthogonal Rotation to Congruence. *Psychometrica*, 1966, 31, pp. 33-42.

Davidson, W.M. and Carroll, J.B., Speed and Level Component in True Limit Scores: A Factor Analysis. *Edu. Psychol. Measmt.*, 1945, 5, pp. 411-428.

Davis, R.B., Item Analysis in Relation to Educational and Psychological Measurement, *Psychol. Bull.* 1952, 49, pp. 97-121.

Dempster, J.J.B., Symposium of Selection of Pupils for Different Types of Secondary Schools: V-The Selector's Point of View. *Brit. J. Educ. Psychol.*, 1948, 18, pp. 1121-133.

Eritsyan, M.S., The Psychological Characteristics of Deductive Reasoning. *(Russ) Voprosy Psikhologii*, 1980, No. 6, pp. 127-130, Abstract taken from *Psychological Abstract*, 1981, 66.

Evans, J.S., Current-Issues in the Psychology of Reasoning. *(France) Bulletin de Psychologie*, 1978-79, 32, pp. 8-14, pp. 643-653. Abstract taken from *Psychological Abstracts*, 1981, 65.

Eysenck, H.J., Critical Notice of Primary Mental Abilities by L.L. Thurstone. *Brit., J., Educ. Psychol.*, 1939, 9, pp. 270-275.

Fan, C.T., Note on Construction of an Item Analysis Table for the High-Low-27 per cent Group Method. *Psychometrika*, 1954, 19, pp. 231-237.

Ferguson, G.A., On Learning and Human Ability. *Canad. J. Psychol.*, 1954, 8, pp. 95-112.

Flangan, J.C., General Considerations in the Selection of Test Items and a Short Method of Estimating the Product-Moment Coefficient from Data at the Tails of the Distribution. *J. of Educ. Psychol.*, 1939, 30, 674-680.

Fruchter, B., The Nature of Verbal Fluency. *Educ. Psychol. Measur.*, 1948, 8, pp. 3-47.

Garrett, H.E., Bryan, A.I. and Perl, R.E., The Age Factor in Mental Organization. *Arch. Psychol.*, N.Y. 1935, No. 176.

Garrett, H.E., A Development Theory of Intelligence. *Amer. Psychologist*, 1946, 1, pp. 372-378.

Green, R.F., Guilford, J.P., Christensen, P.R. and Comrey, A.L., A Factor-Analytic Study of Reasoning Abilities. *Psychometrika*, 1953, 18, No. 2. pp. 135-160.

Guilford, J.P., New Standards for Test Evaluation. *Educ. Psychol. Measur.*, 1946, 6, pp. 427-438.

Guilford, J.P., Christensen, P.R., Kettner, N.W., Green, R.F. and Hertzka, A.F., A Factor-Analytic Study of Navy Reasoning Tests with the Air Force Air-Crew Classification Battery. *Edu. Psychol. Measur.*, 1954, 16, pp. 301-325.

Guilford, J.P., The Structure of Intellect. *Psychol. Bull.*, 1956, 53, pp. 267-293.

Guilford, J.P., The Faces of Intellect. *Amer. Psychologist*, 1959, 14, pp. 469-497.

Guilford, J.P., Thrustone's Primary Mental Abilities and Structure of Intellect Abilities. *Psychol., Bull.*, 1972, 77, No. 2, pp. 129-143.

Holzinger, K.J. and Harman, H.H., Comparison of Two Factorial Analysis. *Psychometrica*, 1938, 3, pp. 45-60.

Hotelling, H., Analysis of a Complex of Statistical Variables into Principal Components. *J. of Educ. Psychol.*, 1933, 24, pp. 417-441 and 498-520.

Kaiser, H.F., The Varimax Criterion for Analytic Rotation in Factor Analysis. *Psychometrika*, 1958, 23, pp, 187-200.

Kaiser, H.F., Computer Programmes for Varimax Rotation in Factor Analysis. *Educ. and Psychol., Measur.*, 1959, 19, pp. 413-420.

Kaiser, H.F., The Application of Electronic Computers to Factor Analysis. *Educ. Psychol. Measur.*, 1966, 20, pp. 141-151.

Kelley, T.L., The Selection of Upper and Lower Groups for the Validation of Test Items. *J. of Educ. Psychol.* 1939, 30, pp. 17-24.

Kenney, P.B., A note on the Formal Requirement for Factorial Studies of Differentiation of Abilities with Age. *Aust. J. Educ.*, 1958, pp. 121-122.

Kettner, N.W., Guilford, J.P. and Christensen, P.R., A Factor-Analytic Investigation of the Factor Called General Reasoning. *Educ. and Psychol. Measure.* Vol. XVI, 16, 1956, pp. 438-453.

Kettner, N.W., Guilford J.P. and Christensen, P.R., A Factor-Analytic Study Across the Domains of Reasoning, Creativity and Evaluation. *Psychol. Monogr., General & Applied*, No. 9, 1959, 73, pp. 1-31.

Merrifield, P.R., Guilford, J.P., Christensen, P.R. and Frick, J.W., The Role of Intellectual Factor in Problem Solving. *Psychol. Monogr.* 1962, 76, No. 10.

Mitchell, J.C., Jr., A Comparison of the Factorial Structure of Cognitive Functions for the High and Low Status Groups. *J. Educ. Psychol.*, 1956, 47, pp. 397-414.

Neuhaus, J.O. and Wrigley, C., The Quartimax Method. *Brit. J. Statist. Psychol.*, 7, pp. 81-91.

Noble, Clyde E., Philosophy of Science in Contemporary Psychology. *Psycho. Reports*, 1947 (Dec.).

Rimoldi, H.J.A., Study of Some Factors related to Intelligence. *Psychometrika*, 1948, 13, pp. 27-46.

Rimoldi, H.J.A., The Central Intellective Factor. *Psychometrica*, 1951, 16, pp. 75-101.

Saunders, D.R., A Computer Program to find the Best-Fitting Orthogonal Factors for a Given Hypothesis. *Psych.* 1960, 25, pp. 199-205.

Sharma, K.N., Analysis of a Test of Reasoning Ability. *J. of Educ. & Psycho.*, 1960, 18, No. 4, pp. 228-240.

Shulman, Lee S., Psychological Controversies in the Teaching of Science and Mathematics. *Science Teacher*, 1968, 35, pp. 34-38, pp. 89-90. Reproduced from M.D. Glock, Guiding Learning. New York: John Willey, 1971.

Slater, P. and Bennett, E., The Development of Spatial Judgement. *Occup. Psychol.*, Vol. 17, 1943.

Spearmon, C., General Intelligence Objectively Determined and Measured. *Amer. J. Psychol.*, 1904, 15, pp. 201-293.

Stephenson, W., Tetrad-Differences for Non-Verbal Sub-Tests. Tetrad-Differences for Verbal Sub-tests Relative to Non-Verbal Subtests. *J. Educ. Psychol.*, 1931, 22, pp. 167-185; 255-267 and 334-350.

Taylor, C.W., A Factorial Study of Fluency in Writing. *Psychometrica*, 1947, 12, pp. 232-262.

Thorndike, E.L. *et al.*, Intelligence and its Measurement: A Symposium. *J. of Educ. Psychol.*, 1921, 12, pp. 123-147; 195-216 and 271-275.

Thurstone, L.L., Primary Mental Abilities. *Psychometr., Mongr.* 1938, No. 1.

Thurstone, L.L. and T.E., Factorial Studies of Intelligence. *Psychometr., Mongr.*, 1941, 2.

Thurstone, L.L., The Effects of Selection in Factor Analysis. *Psychometrika*, 1945, 10, pp. 165-198.

Vernon, M.D., Different Types of Perceptual Ability. *Brit. J. Psychol.*, 1947, 38, pp. 79-89.

Wheeler, D., Studies in the Development of Reasoning in School Children. *Brit. J. Stat. Psychol.*, 1958, 11, pp. 137-159.

Wilson, R.C., Guilford, J.P. Christensen, P.R. and Lewis, D.J., A Factor-Analytic Study of Creative Thinking Abilities, *Psychometrica*, 1954, 19, pp. 297-311.

Zimmerman, W.S., A Revised Orthogonal Solution for Thurstone's Original Primary Mental Abilities Test Battery, *Psychometrica*, 1953, 18, pp. 77-93.

Reports and Documents

Adavel, S.B., The Third Indian Year Book of Education. New Delhi: NCERT, 1968.

Adkins, D.C., and Lyerly, S.B., Factor Analysis of Reasoning Tests. The University of North Carolina, 1952.

Barlow, H.B., Inductive Inference, Coding, Perception and Language Perception, Vol. 3(2). Lab, Cambridge, 1974, pp. 123-134.

Burt, C., Annual Report of the London County Council's Psychologist, 1915.

Daniel, Mark, A Factorial Study of Reasoning Tests, Technical Report 1982-86. Johnson O' Connor Research Foundations, Chicago II, Human Engineering Lab., Sept., 82.

Davis, F.P., Item Analysis Data, Their Computation Interpretation and Use in Test Construction Harvard Education papers, Number 2, Cambridge, Mass., Graduate School of Education, Harvard University, 1946.

Framework, Curriculum for the Ten-year School–A Framework. New Delhi: NCERT, 1975.

Framework, National Curriculum for Primary and Secondary Education – A Framework. New Delhi: NCERT, 1986.

Framework, National Curriculum for Elementary and Secondary Education – A Framework (Revised Version). New Delhi: NCERT, 1988.

Guilford, J.P. and Lacey, J.I., Printed Classification Tests. Washington: Air Forces Aviation Psychology. Research Program, Reports No. 5, 1947.

Guilford, J.P., Comrey, A.L., Green, R.F., and Christensen, P.R., A Factor Analytic Study of Reasoning Abilities. I. Hypothesis and Description of Tests. Los Angles: Rep. Psychol. Lab., No. 1, Univer. of Southern California, 1950.

Guilford, J.P., Green, R.F., and Christen, P.R., A Factor-Analytic Study of Reasoning Abilities. II. Administration of Tests and Analysis of Results. Los Angles: Rep. Psychol. Lab., No. 3, Univer. of Southern California, 1951.

Guilford, J.P., Green, R.F., Christensen, P.R., Hertzka, A.F., and Kettner, N.W., A Factor-Analytic Study of Navy Reasoning Tests with the Air Force Air Crew Classification Battery. Log Angles: Reports from the Psychol. Lab., No. 6, Univer. of Southern California, 1952.

Guilford, J.P., Kettner, N.W., and Christensen, P.R., A Factor-Analytic Study Across the Domains of Reasoning Creativity and Evaluation: I Hypothesis and Description of Test. Los Angles: Rep. Psychol. Lab., No. 11, Univer. of Southern California, 1954.

Guilford, J.P., Kettner, N.W., Christensen, P.R., A Factor-Analytic Study Across the Domains of Reasoning, Creativity and Evaluation: II Administration of Tests and Analysis of Results. Los Angles: Rep. Psychol. Lab., No. 11, Univer. of Southern California, 1956.

Guilford, J.P., A Revised Structure of Intellect. Los Angles: Rep. Psychol. Lab., No. 19, Univer. of Southern California, 1957.

Munoz, C.M., A Logical Approach to the Testing of Deductive and Inductive Abilities. Washington D.C.: Bureau of Policies and Standards, Technical Study Civil Service Commission, July 1977.

Marks, A., Guilford, J.P. and Merrifield, P.R., A Study of Military Leadership in Relation to Selected Intellectual Factors. Los Angles: Rep. Psychol. Lab., No. 21, Univer. of Southern California, 1959.

National Policy on Education. New Delhi: Ministry of Education, Publication No. 832, Government of India, 1968.

National Policy on Education. New Delhi: Ministry of Human Resource Development. Government of India (Deptt. of Education), May, 1986.

Northrop. Lois, C. The Definition and Measurement of Reasoning, Washington D.C.: U.S. Civil Service Commission, Personnel Research and Development Center, 1977 (Aug.) No. 77-10.

Report of the University Education Commission (1948-1949) (Vol. I). New Delhi: Ministry of Education. Government of India, Reprint, 1962.

Report of the Secondary Education Commission (1952-53). New Delhi: Government of India Press, Sixth Reprint, 1965.

Report of the Education Commission (1964-66), Education and National Development (First Edition), New Delhi: Ministry of Education, Government of India, 1966.

Sternberg, R.J., Towards a Unified Componential Theory of Human Reasoning. New Haven. Conn.: Deptt. of Psychol., Technical Report, No. 4, Yale Univ., April, 1978.

Vernon, P.E., Intelligence Testing 1928-1978. What Next? The Scottish Council for Research in Education, 1979.

Ph.D. Thesis

Bala, G.A., A Factor Analysis of Reasoning Ability of 13, 14 and 15 year old children studying in Delhi Higher Secondary Schools. New Delhi: JMI, Unpublished Ph.D. Thesis, 1977.

Butt, A.S., The Differentiation of Reasoning Abilities at Adolescence. London: University of London, Ph.D. Thesis, 1957.

Chauhan, C.P.S., An Evaluation of Achievement in Algebra of Class IX students in Delhi Schools with Reference to categories of Guilford's Structure of Intellect Model. New Delhi., JMI, Ph.D. Thesis, 1982.

Chhikara, M.S., An Investigation into the Relationship of Reasoning Abilities with Achievement of Concepts in Life Sciences. New Delhi: JMI, Unpublished Ph.D. Thesis, 1982.

Cox, W.F., Developmental Aspects of Inductive and Deductive Reasoning. Florida State University, Ph.D. Thesis, 1972.

Dorminey, R.J.D., An Investigation of Interaction Between Selected Aptitudes and Two Methods of Presenting a Unit in Secondary School Mathematics. University of Georgia, Ph.D. Thesis, 1972.

Ross, G.R., A Factor Analytic Study of Inductive Reasoning Tests. Florida State University, Ph.D. Thesis, 1975.

Shah, P.G., Construction and Standardization of Verbal Reasoning Test for Students of Standard VI and Standard VII in Saurashtra, Sau. Univer., Ph.D. Educ. 1981.

Sharma, N., A Study of Mental Organization in School Going Children. Agra Univer., Ph.D., Psy. 1980.

Singh, S., An Investigation into the Interrelationship Between Achievement of Certain Concepts of Physical Chemistry and Cognition and Convergent Production of Semantic Classes, Relations and Implications of the Morphological Model of Structure of Intelligence. New Delhi: JMI, Ph.D. Edu., (Unpublished) 1987.

Tewari, A.D., An Investigation into the Interrelationship Between Measures of Selected Guilford's SI Factors and Set Concepts Achievement of Secondary Level Students of Delhi State. New Delhi: JMI, Unpublished Ph.D. Thesis, 1985.

Tyagi, R.C., Factorial Analysis of SI Abilities in Relation with Achievement in Physics New Delhi: JMI, Ph.D. Edu., (unpublished), 1987.

Miscellaneous

Edwards, P., *The Encyclopedia of Philosophy* (Vol. II) New York: Macmillan, 1967.

Fan, C.T., *Item Analysis Tables*. Princeton: Educational Testing Service, 1952.

Guilford, J.P., *et al. Studies of Aptitudes of High Level Personnel*. Los Angles: Univer. of Southern California, Reports from the Psychol. Lab., 1950-57, No. 1-20.

Guilford, J.P., *New Frontiers of Testing in the Discovery and Development of Human Talent*. Los Angles: In Seventh Annual Western Regional Conference on Testing problems. Educational Testing Service, 1958.

Harper Jr. A.E., Dasgupta, B. and Sengal, S.P., *Item Analysis Chart and Instructions*. Delhi: Manasayan, 1962.

Laird, C.G., *Webster's New Word Thesaurus*. New York: Simson & Schuster, 1971.

Mitra, S.K. and Kumar, K., in M.B. Buch's, *A Survey of Research in Education*. Baroda: M.S. University, Faculty of Educ. & Psychol., 1974.

Natarajan, V., *Monograph on Sampling – Free Item Analysis for Universities*. New Delhi: Association of Indian Universities, 1987.

Nie, N.H. Hull., C.H. Jenkins, J.H., Steinbrenner, K. and Bent, D.H., *Statistical Package for the Social Sciences* (2nd Ed.) New York: McGraw-Hill, 1975.

Raven, J.C., *Standard Progressive Matrices – Sets A, B, C, D and E*. London: H.K. Lewis, 1958.

Raven, J.C. *et al., Manual for Raven's Progressive Matrices and Vocabulary Scales* – Section-3, Standard Progressive Matrices. London: H.K. Lewis, 1983.

INDEX